THE
SIMPLE
ART OF
SCRAPBOOKING

THE SIMPLE ART OF SCRAPBOOKING

Tips, Techniques, and 30 Special Album Ideas
For Creating Memories That Last a Lifetime

THE SCRAPBOOK GUILD

A Seth Godin Production

A DELL TRADE PAPERBACK

A DELL TRADE PAPERBACK
Published by
Dell Publishing
a division of
Bantam Doubleday Dell Publishing Group, Inc.
1540 Broadway
New York, New York 10036

Book design by Rose Gonnella and Joseph Konopka
Illustrations by Rose Gonnella

Library of Congress Cataloging in Publication Data
The simple art of scrapbooking : tips, techniques, and 30 special album ideas for creating memories that last a lifetime / the Scrapbook Guild.
p.   cm.
ISBN 0-440-50839-8
1. Photograph albums. 2. Photographs—Conservation and restoration. 3. Scrapbooks.
I. Scrapbook Guild (U.S.)
TR465.S56   1998
745.593—dc21
98-7683
CIP

Printed in the United States of America

Published simultaneously in Canada

November 1998
10 9 8 7 6 5 4 3 2 1
FFG

For our wonderful families;
Reason enough to create a thousand scrapbooks

Acknowledgments

Special thanks for sharing their very special scrapbooks to Flynn Berry, Marvin Davis, Penny Delany, Lisa DiMona, Linda Lee Johnson, Jacques Pépin, Isabel Carter Stewart, and Elizabeth Winship.

Thank-you to the gang at Seth Godin Productions, Linda Carbone, Jennifer Cecil, Lisa DiMona, Seth Godin, Erin Lyons, Jason Mandell, Sarah Silbert, Karen Watts, and Ann Weinerman, for being the kind of colleagues who inspire an office scrapbook.

Much gratitude and thanks to Kean University of New Jersey design department faculty, Denise Anderson, Martin Holloway, Robin Landa, and Alan Robbins for their advice and inspiration, Kean alumnus, Dan Medina for his wonderfully "fishy" ideas, and Kean design student, David Ellman for his creative contribution to the cover of the team sports scrapbook.

Heartfelt thanks for all the "scrappy" creativity and efforts of Thomas Cannon, Larry Coffin, Robin Dellabough, Josephine Gonnella, Ellen Matlach Hassell, Russell Hassell, Franco Holahan, Joseph Konopka (Big Shot), Marina, Sylvia, Raye and Bill Leith, Kris Philipps, and Angela Plunkett.

THE SIMPLE ART OF SCRAPBOOKING

CONTENTS

THE
SIMPLE
ART OF
SCRAPBOOKING

Jacques Pépin is the host of award-winning cooking shows on national public television, a master chef, former New York Times columnist, and author of 16 cookbooks. Born and raised in a town near Lyon in France, he moved to the United States in 1959 after serving as personal chef to French heads of state, including Charles de Gaulle. He has worked on books, television, and videotapes with Julia Child and James Beard, although his most recent show, Jacques Pépin's Kitchen: Cooking with Claudine *was his hands-down favorite. (Claudine is his daughter.) Between appearances on* The Today Show, Good Morning America, *and David Letterman, Jacques has found time to produce a line of specialty food products; copper cookware manufactured by Bourgeat, Inc.; and kitchen textiles featuring his own designs. A founder of the American Institute of Wine and Food, he is Dean of Special Programs at the French Culinary Institute in New York and an adjunct faculty member at Boston University.*

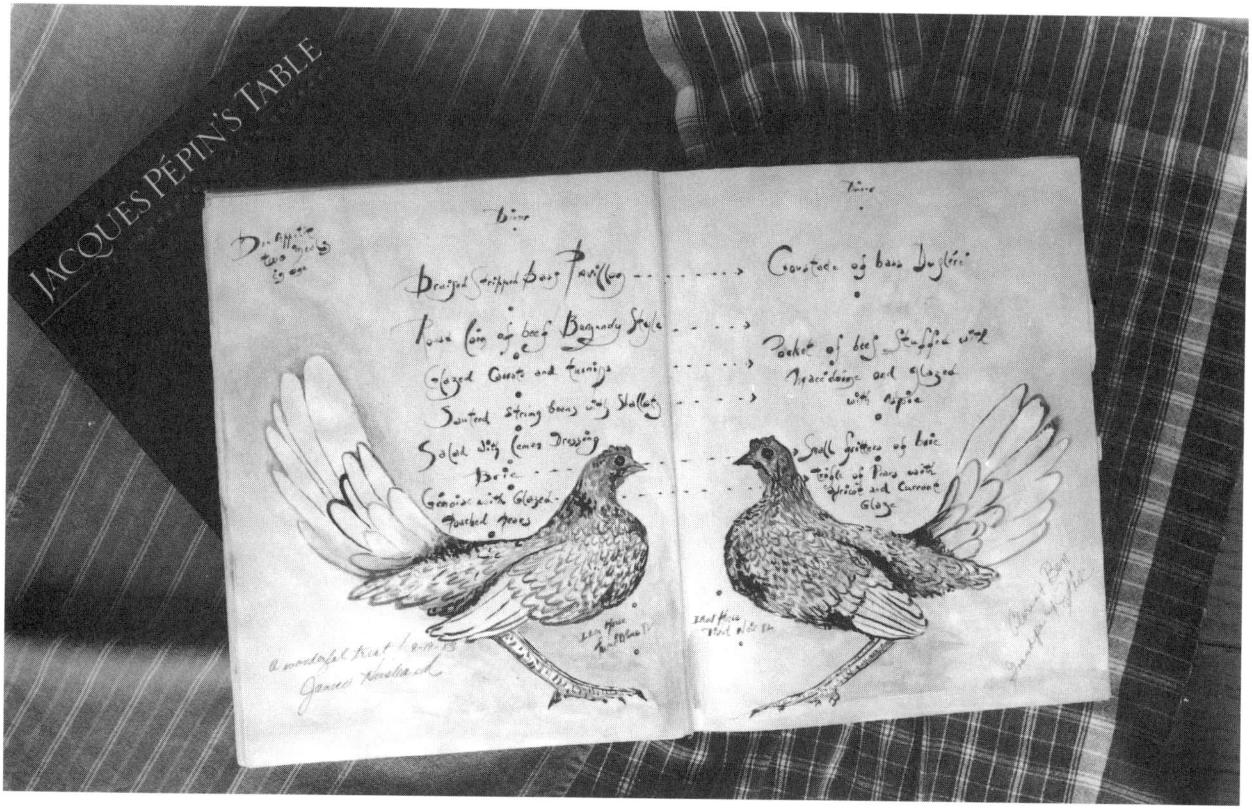
JACQUES PÉPIN'S TABLE

The Scrapbook Guild

Scrapbook Guild Members

Rose Gonnella, Designer and Illustrator

Rose is an artist, illustrator, writer, and educator.

She has exhibited her drawings both nationally and internationally for 15 years. Her work is included in the permanent collections of the National Museum of American Art, Washington, D.C., The Museum of Art and Archaeology, Columbia, Missouri, The Sara Roby Foundation, and other public and private collections. The Jane Haslem Gallery in Washington, D.C., and The Main Street Gallery in Nantucket, Massachusetts, exhibit her work.

Rose is currently Associate Professor in the Design Department at Kean University in Union, New Jersey, where she teaches illustration, computer graphics, and design.

The artist spends her summers on Nantucket, drawing and writing.

Patricia Dreame Wilson, Writer

Patricia Dreame Wilson has enjoyed 20 years of experience as a writer and editor, including the conceptualizing and editing of four volumes of *American Country Christmas* for Time Warner's Oxmoor House. Currently a contributing editor for *Mary Engelbreit's Home Companion* magazine, Patricia is working on her own book, *The Fairy Seasons,* a children's book of crafts, nature surprises, and enchantments.

She lives in Atlanta, Georgia, with her husband, novelist Charles McNair, and their four-year-old daughter Bonnie Dreame.

Charlotte Lyons, Photo Stylist

Charlotte has written eight books in the popular home decorating and crafts series with illustrator Mary Engelbreit and photographer Barbara Martin. Her work as a designer and writer has also been featured in *Country Living, Mary Engelbreit's Home Companion* magazine and in various Oxmoor House publications, such as *Scrapcrafts for All Occasions.*

Marie Nuccitelli, Scrapbook Guild

A consultant and professional scrapbooker, Marie lives in Salt Lake City, Utah, where she has been scrapbooking since she was a child. She writes articles for scrapbook magazines and teaches scrapbook classes as well as posting her sample pages on the Internet to share with other enthusiasts.

Jennia Hart, Scrapbook Guild

A product and business consultant for scrapbooking manufacturers, Jennia has helped develop several well-known scrapbooking products. She writes articles and creates scrapbook pages for scrapbooking publications. She develops and maintains The Scrapbooking Idea Network (http://www.scrapbooking.com), the original and largest scrapbooking community on the Internet.

She lives in Oxnard, California with her husband Mark and her four-year-old son Drew.

Jody Williams, Scrapbook Guild

Jody received an MFA in printmaking and
since then has been producing work through
her company, Flying Paper Press. A visiting
artist at many crafts centers and a juror of the
American Craft Council Fair, she also teaches
at the Minneapolis College of Art and Design,
the Minnesota Center for Book Arts, and the
University of Minnesota. Her artists' books,
prints, and paper works have been exhibited
and collected nationally, as well as in Europe.

A distinguished patron *of music and founder of the music division of the Library of Congress, Elizabeth Sprague Coolidge had an auditorium for chamber music built in Washington, D.C. She sponsored music and musicians from around the world and would invite chamber music groups to perform for a fee in Washington and then for free at universities and schools. Both performers and audiences benefited by the result: some of the best chamber music in the world at that time. This is the cover of her Victorian scrapbook.*

INTRODUCTION

Do not fear mistakes—there are none.

— Miles Davis

Why Make Scrapbooks?

In our busy lives, bombarded by the demands of today's high-tech world, we have so little time for the things that really matter. Scrapbooking keeps us connected to what is important in life—family, friends, and the experiences we share with them. The simple act of pasting photographs and jotting down impressions in a book is a relaxing way to record history. By taking bits and pieces from our lives and putting them together in one place, we celebrate our existence and create something timeless in a world where there seems to be no time at all.

And speaking of time, the wonderful thing about scrapbooking is that, like quilting, which can be done one block at a time, scrapbooking can be done one page at a time. When that page is finished, possibly after one sitting, you have something complete. It is a boost to your creativity that everyone around you can understand, enjoy, and appreciate.

Many of us, whether we freely admit it or not, have a sentimental streak. We can't bear to throw away a handmade card from a special friend or our child's first stick-figure drawing. Scrapbooking gives us a practical way to preserve tangible memories from days gone by, and pulling together these various elements can be a very creative process. Scrapbooks also give us a usable resource, showing the places we've been—(What was the name of that cute little B & B we stayed in that night?)—the things we've seen—(What museum was that painting in?)—not to mention the people we were.

Organizing and protecting your priceless photographs may be the most important reason to scrapbook. Right now, how many of your precious photos and negatives lie scattered around the house—in boxes in the attic, drawers in the guest room, or even stuck in harmful plastic "magnetic" photo albums? By using the best materials for your photos and mementos, you'll have a family album (or two) that displays your history clearly and safely . . . for many years to come.

A Story to Tell

We all have a story to tell. A thousand stories, really. There's little Bonnie's first year when she grew so fast and charmed so many. Remember the once-in-a-lifetime family vacation to search for traces of your ancestors in Europe? Or the summers spent at grandmother's cottage on the coast of Maine? What about your college years when you met your life-long friends and learned more than calculus? And how can you forget the family myth you've heard a hundred times about the sweet-sounding violin your grandfather made?

Every life has many unique stories, but few of us take the time to write them down. That's really a shame, because in an important way we honor our lives—our families, friends, and accomplishments—through the stories we tell. To preserve those tales for generations to come is an act of love. A scrapbook of family pictures and mementos captures the narrative of our daily lives and commemorates our friendships, our successes, our family ties, our interests. Scrapbooks highlight the landmark moments, both large and small.

In your hands you can hold memories—a Valentine made by your four year old, the ticket stub and program from your first Broadway play, a picture of your father wearing a funny hat, a letter from your favorite aunt. These mementos, rather than being stuck haphazardly in boxes under the bed, can be organized by theme and category to tell a richly detailed story—page by beautiful page.

Elizabeth Winship, of Lincoln, Massachusetts, has written an advice column for teens since 1964. Called "Ask Beth," the column is syndicated nationally in newspapers such as The Boston Globe. She is also the coauthor of a book called Risky Times: How to Be AIDS-Smart and Stay Healthy. This scrapbook belonged to her grandmother, Elizabeth Sprague Coolidge, and contains her collection of Victorian ephemera, which, as you can see, she pasted sparingly and caringly on each page.

The History of Scrapbooks

Our cabin measured 16 x 20 feet in the clear. The logs were chinked and painted with clay. The floor was of earth, beaten hard and smooth, a box cupboard held our stack of dishes and cooking utensils. Beside it stood the churn. The flour barrel was converted into a center-table where on reposed the family Bible and photograph album with their white lace covers.

— Albert Jerome Dickson,
Covered Wagon Days, 1929

With the introduction of photography, the first photograph albums appeared. From the beginning, they were family treasures. Blank-paged books, called autograph books, brimmed with pictures of family members and friends who would write a little inscription on the page. Later, around 1860, specialty albums held the popular "carte-de-visite" or visiting card, a card-backed photograph of a visitor, a celebrity, or a famous place. "Cabinet cards," which were larger cartes, became popular in the late 1860s.

Of course, even before paper photographs grew to be the rage, photographers captured faces and personalities in daguerreotypes, images printed on a silver or silver-plated copper plate. These striking slips of silver bore rich frames with gilt mats and fit into cases of finely embossed leather. The miniature books surely stand as predecessors of later albums.

The first photograph albums had standard, pre-cut openings to hold carte-de-visite and cabinet cards. They resembled the cherished family bibles of the time, with ornate leather covers, gilt-edged pages, and a decorative brass clasp. In the late 1800s, other covers of celluloid or velvet with tiny inset mirrors became available.

In the early 20th century, albums began to be seen as a more informal, individual form of expression. These books carried blank pages of pale grey or green at first, until around 1903, when black was most commonly used. Titles and descriptions could be penned in white ink on these black pages for dramatic effect. Collectors pasted pictures directly to the pages or held them in place with photo corners.

During the Victorian era, exquisitely colorful printed papers, often referred to as "scraps," became available through a labor-intensive printing process known as chromolithography. Ladies saved valentines, birth and wedding announcements, calling cards, calendars, even cigar box labels for a time, treasuring them for their intensely beautiful colors and charming scenes. From use of these scraps came our modern term—scrapbook.

Starting in Victorian times up until the 1950s, black-paged scrapbooks were the most common. These commonly featured a hodgepodge of photographs and mementos from throughout the years, all collected in one book. After World War II, proud collectors deemed single special events, such as a wedding, the birth of a baby, or a family vacation, worthy of an entire album. In this way, individual storybook photo albums grew to be popular.

Now at the close of the 20th century, a new scrapbooking phenomenon has sprung up. From your local craft store to the Internet, scrapbook information and supplies abound. A federal holiday celebrates the first Saturday in May as National Scrapbook Day. No longer are we content to buy an album at the local drugstore, slap down a few pictures with school glue, and call it a scrapbook. Today's scrapbookers are inspired to use archival materials, organize photos and mementos around themes, and create original exciting page layouts. As a result, with roots in the birth of photography, scrapbooking has a bright future today all its own.

What's to Come

With *The Simple Art of Scrapbooking* we give you hands-on advice and tons of information to help you begin telling your story right away.

In *Part One: How to Get Started*, you'll find out about necessary materials and supplies, how to set up a work space, and suggestions on choosing themes. You'll also learn important archival information that will help ensure your precious memories last for generations to come.

In *Part Two: Make a Scrapbook*, you'll read about journal writing, cropping, decoration and design, and preserving your assorted memorabilia.

In *Part Three: Tips and Techniques*, Scrapbook Guild members offer their favorite secrets on everything from organization to motivation.

Part Four: Thirty Scrapbook Ideas describes unique projects, from daily life to magical moments. These include suggested materials, illustrations of sample layouts, and lettering ideas for creating scrapbooks on fishing and friendship, collections and cooking.

In *Part Five: Scrapbook Socials*, you'll discover ways to share your enthusiasm for scrapbooking with others in parties and clubs, cruises, or family get-togethers.

Part Six: Resource Section is a comprehensive and accurate list of the many resources available to scrapbookers—from suppliers to books and Internet sites.

Reasons to Scrapbook Today

We all have the urge to carve out our own piece of history. A scrapbook of your life may not be the history taught at your local high school, but it's even better—a personal history that has a resonant intimacy.

In taking the time to make scrapbooks, we also pass on family traditions and values. We teach our children the importance of family research. Even families fragmented by geography or divorce reestablish a sense of tradition through albums that record the heritage of ancestors.

Within the covers of a family album lie a range of emotions—shouts of joy, tears of defeat, the strength of courage, the power of love, and sometimes lots of just plain silliness. To create a scrapbook is to create a gift of love. Simply put, scrapbooking is loving and giving. Hours of sorting and planning, cutting and pasting most certainly are motivated primarily by love—love of family, love of self, love of tradition, love of the creative instinct. In the expression of that love comes a gift that will last your lifetime—and longer.

May this book bring you closer to telling your story and the story of your family through the delightful and important craft of scrapbooking.

Florence Carter Johnson (1906–1967) kept this scrapbook while she attended Philadelphia High School for Girls. She herself became a teacher and taught for 36 years in Philadelphia public schools. Although her parents were a postal clerk and a seamstress, they managed to buy land and build a cottage in Nantucket, where the family summered beginning in 1926.

Florence's daughter is Isabel Carter Stewart, the national executive director of Girls, Inc., a nonprofit organization with 350,000 girls at 900 sites around the country. She was also the first lady of Spelman College while her husband served as its president for ten years. Isabel offers these pages in tribute to her ancestors' undaunted spirit, perseverance, and determination to lead full and productive lives even under the most restrictive and segregated of circumstances.

PART ONE:

HOW TO GET STARTED

What we call the beginning is often the end
And to make an end is to make a beginning
The end is where we start from

— T.S. Eliot

Where Do I Begin?

At first, it may be overwhelming to think about starting a scrapbook. Aging pictures lie about the house in drawers, boxes, and trunks. Family letters and cherished pieces of memorabilia hide in dusty corners of the attic. And, of course, none of these rare personal treasures carry labels or dates.

Where do you begin?

If you want to build bedrock confidence, it helps to gather a few supplies and do a little additional planning up front before you paste down those first smiling faces. Some scrapbookers like to make lists, gather materials, revise lists, do trial pages, look around and think, gather some more, and then glue!

The single most important thing to remember is the easiest lesson in the book—have fun. Let scrapbooking be a joy. That joy is contagious, and the bug will likely jump from you to your family and friends, when they see how much you love what you're discovering. Enjoy the process, enjoy the mess, enjoy the finished book. You'll be making wonderful memories . . . and wonderful scrapbooks too.

Keeping It Safe

If you plan to spend the time, energy, and money required to make a scrapbook, consider the materials you'll be using. Try to buy only archival materials. It sounds preposterous, but it's possible that the mix of substances that you bring together in your book—photos, newspaper clippings, family records, even pressed flowers—might cause peculiar chemical combinations. Left to time, these processes could damage the artifacts you've tried so hard to preserve for posterity.

If it is unbearable to imagine someone might open your keepsake scrapbook in ten years to find the pictures of Grandma and Grandpa ruined, take heart. The good news is that there are many safe products available. They can be purchased from specialty stores or catalogs that supply reliable archival quality products. (See the *Resource Section* for a comprehensive list.) These items might be more expensive than similar ones sold in discount stores, but the investment will assure you that your scrapbook will survive for generations to come.

When searching for archival materials, here are a few terms to remember:

- *Acid-free paper has been treated to neutralize or remove the acids that are present in wood-pulp papers. Acid can react with other chemicals present in photos and mementos and cause untimely deterioration. Avoid too much alkaline as well. You want scrapbook papers and other products to be pH neutral and stable, so that the pH balance does not fluctuate over time. Acid-free paper is both neutral and stable. In fact, it is so common now that many manufacturing companies don't state "acid-free" on the package. Call a local paper company for a supplier near you. Almost all Hammermill products are acid-free.*

- *Buffered or alkaline paper is treated with a coating of calcium carbonate to absorb and neutralize acid. This is beneficial for countering the acidic nature of oils from fingers, or when keepsakes, such as highly acidic newspaper clippings, are added to your scrapbook.*

- *Lignin-free paper has been processed to eliminate all but an insignificant trace of the acidic part of the wood pulp, called lignin. Papers that are both acid–free and lignin–free are the highest quality and can be expected to last more than 200 years.*

- *Inert plastics are pH neutral and stable so they do not emit gases that can fade photographs. There are many safe plastics you can choose, including mylar polyester, polypropylene, and polyethylene. Mylar is the choice of serious archivists. It comes in thin sheets, rolls, and envelopes that protect a scrapbook page. You find polypropylene and polyethylene most commonly in sheet protectors, which hold a scrapbook page or two in a pocket. Polypropylene is clear, while polyethylene is frosted. A surprisingly easy way to test the safety of a plastic is just to smell it. Vinyl, or polyvinyl chloride (PVC), has a strongly noticeable odor—not safe for storing photographs.*

- *Magnetic albums have self-adhesive pages made of PVC plastic that breaks down and gives off harmful gases. These eventually destroy photographs sealed within. Photos should never be stored in this type of album. If you have some stored this way now and you treasure them, they should be removed as soon as possible. (See Scrapbook Makeover on page 69 for tips on how to remove pictures.)*

Now that you're archivally savvy, you can make many important decisions about your project. For certain types of scrapbooks of long-term historical value, like family heritage albums, archival materials always make the best choice. But when you see all the multitudes of scrapbook materials that are now available, you may decide to throw caution to the winds and put together a quick, more temporary album just for fun—a scrapbook to welcome someone new to your neighborhood, for example. If you're using duplicate photographs or color photocopies, go right ahead. Enjoy the spontaneity!

Choosing Different Themes Or Occasions

Every day is a memory in the making and completely worthy of savoring in a scrapbook. Whether a scrapbook celebrates ordinary, everyday occurrences or highlights a single person's life, the love that went into creating it shines through. Any event and any individual is a potential theme.

For your first book, you could choose to honor an individual. (Why not yourself?) Or start with a child's album, a vacation scrapbook, or a family scrapbook. Themes like these make it easy to get started. As you become more proficient with arranging your ideas and photos, you could tackle a more complex family history, a collector's scrapbook, or a tribute to certain best friends or siblings.

Look through the *Scrapbook Ideas*, beginning on page 97, for specific themes to get you going. Does anything here strike your fancy? Don't hesitate—if you jump right in, you'll begin learning more than you ever thought possible about scrapbooking. Mainly, you'll learn how much fun it can be.

Start by looking through your pictures. Examine the ideas that begin to roll around in your head and watch for themes or occasions you wish to single out. As you sort, keep a few photo boxes at the ready. Drop one kind of idea here, another there. Soon, a "big picture" will come to mind.

You may also wish to sort chronologically. Arrange by decade first, then year by year to help keep it manageable. Another approach is to spread out all the photos you've collected over the past year and see what sort of themes emerge directly from the whole array of images.

Organization

No matter which themes catch your fancy, organization right from the start is your key to a pleasant experience and a wonderful finished product. Although the word organization may send shivers up your spine, it really makes the work of scrapbooking so much easier when, like oil, just a little is applied at the right time, in the right places.

First, gather all your materials together—and we mean everything. Check framed pictures around the house. Make copies of relatives' pictures that you've always meant to borrow. Pull out old photo albums. Play Miss Marple and make a thorough sweep of likely sources for the treasures you really want.

Next, look over all the photos and memorabilia, and consider their order in your book.

Your arrangement can be chronological, but it certainly doesn't have to be. Just be open to whatever emerges and speaks to you from that mountain of material out of which you will shape your project.

Once you've decided on an organization method, get some archival photo boxes, accordion envelopes, or manila envelopes for the sorting process. Label them according to category, theme, or person and you'll have a quick, safe place to store your materials as you go along.

Make a Timeline

Whether or not you choose to arrange your scrapbook chronologically, making a timeline can be useful. For many, the framework of time itself—the spreadsheet of dates and years, birthdays and graduations all in a neat calendar grid—provides a perfect organizational tool. If this system works for you, congratulations—you're ready to advance to GO. Remember, there aren't any hard-and-fast rules in scrapbooking. What you want to discover is a way into your project. For many scrapbookers, a simple timeline unlocks the door.

Negatives

As you organize your pictures, you might consider organizing your negatives as well. Some of the most commonly used photographic papers may begin to fade after only ten years, so you may eventually need to reprint your favorite pictures. If, heaven forbid, something should happen to your scrapbook, at least you'll be able to get your hands on your negatives. If your negatives have been organized, labeled, and filed in an accessible way, your task will be that much easier.

What's the best way to organize negatives? Start by using files made of inert plastics or archival paper files. (See *Keeping It Safe* on page 36 and *Resource Section,* on page 239.)

Or keep your negatives in mylar sleeves in a three-ring binder. There are special markers available at most photo supply stores for labeling negative sleeves. You can label numerically or by event, whichever way makes retrieval easier.

To protect against a fire, flood, or some other natural disaster, consider storing your negatives in a safety deposit box or a fire-safe box. This may seem overly fastidious, but remember that it is impossible to place a value on the only existing photograph of a Civil War-era matriarch or on a photo of a beloved child's first recital.

If you're at all electronically "wired," you might want to look into digital options for storing special negatives. More and more photo shops, for a reasonable fee, will scan negatives and store them on-line or save them on a computer disk. It is also possible to have your album pages scanned onto a disk, so a duplicate will exist. Keep in mind,

though, that the staying power of much of the imagery committed to high-tech archives has yet to be proven. The technology may change so rapidly as to make disks obsolete, or the images may fade in years to come. Only time will tell how cyberspace serves as a substitute attic. But no matter what, some back-up is better than none.

Storage

The question of virtual storage on a computer brings up another issue—the best place to physically warehouse scrapbook materials until you are ready to work with them. All photographs, negatives, and supplies are fragile elements in a world of hard knocks and rough edges. They need extra protection.

Do your heirlooms a favor and immediately eliminate three traditional storage spots—the attic, the basement, and the garage. When you stop to think, it's not hard to understand why.

Linda Lee Johnson is a founding member of the Berkeley Repertory Theater and performed leading roles in major regional theaters and in New York City. Concurrently she studied jewelry making and sculpture. She has made pieces for the stores of the Museum of Modern Art, Alexander Julian, the Guggenheim Museum, Tiffany and Co., and Barneys New York. Linda Lee says, "To make an object deeply personal and enduring, with reverence for life and spirit, with my hands, is my passion. To share the object is my great privilege." A featured designer for Lunt Silversmiths, she lives with her husband, actor James Lally, in SoHo, New York. This page from her professional scrapbook captures the design of a 22 karat gold earring and pendant, from initial sketches to a photograph of the finished pieces. She liked the results so much, the tiny bee is now her trademark. The silver key chain is also by the designer; you can't see the little bee, which is on the rim, along with the word "light" in several languages.

bunny bee

bunny bee

phoebe earring
and pendant   1980

22K

the jewelers trademark
bee with bird motif on
reverse

Paper needs a stable environment. That means it does best in a narrow range of temperatures—between 65 and 70 degrees Fahrenheit—with a relative humidity somewhere around 50 percent. Direct sunlight will inevitably fade and dry photographs, just like window curtains or paint on a car, so try to keep your scrapbook materials well shaded at the same time you keep them cool and dry.

Should you build a special wing on the house? Add a humidor, minus cigars? There's no need for extravagances. A bedroom closet usually serves as a good storage place for photos and negatives, offering the right combination of elements for long-term preservation. If a closet doesn't work, look for a place that's away from windows (to protect from sunlight), on an inside wall (to protect from humidity), and, in general, a spot that's clean, cool, and dry.

Store all your supplies in one convenient spot. If you don't have a permanent place, like a closet or a hutch, consider storage boxes. Choose archival paper boxes for long-term storage. For temporary storage, shallow sweater boxes made of plastic hold lots of materials, and they can easily be stashed under a bed. Supplies—glue, scissors, tape, and such—can be kept in shoebox-size plastic boxes. (See *Buying and Storing Supplies* on page 78 for more storage ideas.)

Many scrapbookers find that office armoires provide an attractive, space-saving solution to scrapbook clutter. These cabinets open to reveal shelves and a fold-down desk. You'll find them in office supply and department stores.

If space is really limited, a roll-away utility cart with drawers is a great way to store all your supplies in one spot. You can roll it to whatever room becomes available.

Where to Scrapbook

Scrapbooking requires a certain amount of space, as you will quickly discover after you spread out all your materials. Where can you go?

Click your ruby heels together three times and repeat, like Dorothy, "There's no place like home." Home for a scrapbook-in-progress means a place where you don't have to clean up after every session—a spot to lay everything out and leave it for days on end, with no threat of disturbance.

If you have a dedicated craft area, count yourself among the blessed. Otherwise, try your dining room table, a kitchen counter, a card table, or even the floor (if you don't have pets or small children). If you don't have a large flat surface, make a portable one—use a sheet of plywood or masonite, for example, to expand an existing coffee table-top space.

Choosing Supplies

The sky's the limit for materials and supplies in this booming craft. With so many options, you may feel confused as to what you really need to buy. How do you decide? Try to focus on the basics. Once you're more experienced, you'll develop a better feel for your own particular style, and the wide array of possibilities won't be so daunting.

The materials you really do need—the "must-have" supplies to get you started—are pretty simple, when you get right down to it.

The Album

You can transform a wide variety of albums, journals, and binders into scrapbooks. The most important thing is to find the book that intuitively appeals to you—the one that inspires you to fill it with personal recollections and mementos.

Make sure that the album has a strong binding, since it will be handled over and over again, with great curiosity and respect, for many years. Again, consider buying an archival album with acid-free, PVC-free, photo-safe pages. (See *Keeping It Safe* on page 36 for complete archival information.) This will ensure maximum preservation quality. Such high-quality albums sometimes even have parchment dividers between pages to protect the photographs from dirt, dust, and natural chemical reactions with album paper or one another.

Check the labels on the albums to see whether they qualify as archival albums. These albums come in many styles and range in price from $10 to a $100 or more.

Other than such a basic consideration, your choice of scrapbook album boils down to aesthetics and cost. You'll want to consider a few practical aspects: Where do you want to display your scrapbook? Do you want it to lie flat or do you want to store it vertically? What types of items will you be gluing to its pages? Different approaches require different sorts of albums.

Here are some options:

- *Expandable-spine albums lie flat, with large pages that can be rearranged. You'll find them excellent for most kinds of scrapbooking, because the large pages give you plenty of room for pictures and journal writing. One drawback—you may run out of pages and find the company no longer stocks that size.*

- *Ring-bound albums or binders lie flat as well, with the added advantage of allowing you to insert additional pages into the album at any point. These are a good choice for most kinds of scrapbooking. A caveat: Make certain that they will close completely and the rings do not pop open on their own. Otherwise, pages might slip out.*

- *Spiral-bound albums lie flat and are available in many sizes. Often, these albums have blank covers, which can be easily personalized. Make sure the binding is made to last. A disadvantage here—you won't be able to rearrange pages or insert new ones.*

- *Postbound albums (sometimes officially called scrapbooks) are oversized albums that lie flat, holding punched pages together with metal posts. Make sure the quality of the paper measures up.*

- *Journals and bookbound albums tend to be smaller, with a spine that must be broken in order for the book to lie flat. They usually work better for written entries than for pictures and photos.*

- *Many specialty albums also grace the shelves of finer stores. Exquisitely made by hand with tooled leather or elegant fabric covers and hand-stitched binding, often opening to reveal handmade paper as well, such albums can turn a simple collection of photos and memories into your own personal* Book of Kells.

Whichever albums you feel drawn to, try to fit the style of the album with the theme you plan for your scrapbook. You may not be able to tell a book by its cover, but try to give your readers at least a hint. A white taffeta cover says "wedding day" very elegantly. A burnished steel cover might provide a hint of something more contemporary for a style-conscious teen.

Paper Basics

Your photos and papers will prove more lasting—and stand out more beautifully—if you choose to mount them initially on a paper background. You can then glue this backdrop to the scrapbook page with your choice of adhesive. (See *Just Stick to It* on page 51 for archival choices.) Such lavish use of paper doubles its importance, so it's worth doing a little footwork to make sure you get the kind and quality you really need.

A handful of basic elements distinguish types of paper: weight, flexibility, texture, color, shine, and pattern. Each element, properly fitted into your grand design, can add immeasurably to the beauty and stability of your scrapbook.

As we've stressed, if you're putting together an album you want to last for generations, make sure that you use only paper that is acid-free and lignin-free. However, there are so many wonderful paper choices out there you may choose to let your creativity dictate the final selection. Once you cross that basic bridge, go ahead and experiment. Papers from all over the world, from all sorts of different trees, plants, and pulps, abound. You can pick and choose the background that will be most appropriate to your theme. The background paper sets the mood and adds emotion to your photos and the overall page layout.

As a general rule, it's best to use a neutral color, like white, cream, taupe, beige, or black, for the background paper. These colors are not as likely to compete with the colors and tones of the photos. More colorful paper can then be added to enhance the layout with photo mats, cut-outs, or stickers.

Texture and weight of paper is another consideration. Cardstock and other heavyweight papers make the best background for lightweight papers and photos. Cardstock can also be used to personalize an album's cover. Cut cardstock to fit the cover, print a decorative title on the cardstock, then glue in place.

Japanese paper, composed of long fibers, is very delicate, light, and absorbent. It looks great under poetic images or more artistic photography, such as landscapes or gardens. In general, lightweight papers fold, cut, and tear easily—they make interesting photo mats and decorative designs in any album.

Wrapping paper, available in an enormous variety of weights, themes, patterns, and colors, makes a fun and interesting background for many layout themes. Wrapping paper, however, is seldom acid-free. Use these papers only occasionally or photocopy your favorites onto acid-free paper.

Cotton papers are made from plant fibers and thus do not contain the acidic wood pulp of regular paper. They are available in a choice of colors, weights, and textures at most stationery or paper supply stores.

You can find stunning handmade papers, imaginatively marbled or dyed, at most art supply and stationery stores. (See page 247 for suppliers.) One-of-a-kind art papers with their unique colors and textures add a subtle elegance to any page.

You can add dimension to your scrapbook pages by mounting layers on top of layers, using various types of paper as a matrix for the images you wish to dramatically present. Just remember, the background paper provides continuity for the entire scrapbook.

Cut It Out

Paper, whether in photographs, pages, or decorations, is such an integral part of scrapbooking that the tools you use to cut the paper are equally important.

Your tool kit might include these items:

* *If you're looking for straight, clean edges, sharp scissors will suit your needs just fine. You'll also be using scissors frequently for trimming papers, cutting out silhouettes as a way of deleting a distracting background, and in cutting out original designs and decorations from specialty papers.*

* *X-Acto craft knives and miniature paper cutters produce perfectly clean edges when cropping photos and trimming photo frames and mats. These can add a highly professional look to what you're doing.*

* *Decorative edge scissors give you zigzags, scallops, and other shapes. These scissors add pizzazz or elegance to a page border, photo mat, or photograph. You can find these in discount, craft, and art supply stores.*

* *Decorative craft punches cut small designs and shapes in your photos and papers. You*

can buy anything from small flying cupids to Cheshire cats, and they bring fun and whimsy to a book. For example, why not use a dinosaur shape to trim photos of a first trip to a natural history museum?

Write This Way, Please

To label your photos and record your memories, writing utensils must be part of your supply kit. But a warning here! Always be sure to use pens or markers that are permanent, water proof, fade-proof, and filled with pigment inks, which are more permanent than dye-based inks. The inks should be acid-free, too, so your pictures won't be damaged by any acidity they might carry. The Kuretake Co., Ltd. has a variety of pens in the ZIG Memory System line, which meet all the archival requirements.

Remember rule one in photos and labeling: Never use a ballpoint pen when writing on the backs of photographs. As many photo-labelers have learned, to their dismay and distress, the pressure used to leave an impression in words on the back will also leave an impression on the front of the photograph. A special photo labeling pen or pencil, such as Blue Stabilo, available at photo supply stores, is best for jotting down names and dates on the backs of pictures.

For adorning your pages with the important facts, fun phrases, or other journal writing, here are some other good choices:

- *Paint markers marry the vibrant colors of paints with the superior control of a small-tipped marker.*

- *Dual felt-tip pens have two ends: a wide tip for titles and brush strokes, and a finer tip for stories and notes.*

- *Metallic gold and silver pens can be especially elegant on a dark surface or for a decorative border design.*

- *Calligraphy markers can be found in all art supply stores, and have an angled tip to add flair and sophistication to your writing.*

- *Gel Rolls have the comfortable, familiar feel of a ballpoint pen, but are filled with archival-quality ink. Pen manufacturer Sacra makes Gel Rolls.*

- *Colored pencils may be the best option, and the simplest, when you're writing a long paragraph, or when you want to add more detail or shading to an illustration.*

- *Decorative chalks or pastels blend colors beautifully and add a soft effect . . . but be careful of smudges and smears. When using chalks or pastels, be sure the facing page is blank or place a decorative sheet of tissue over the decorated page.*

Just Stick to It

It may seem like sticky business, but the glue, tape, or mounting corners you use to attach your pictures and decorations to the album pages really come down to a few simple considerations.

The most important thing about choosing glue is, once again, to make sure that it's acid-free. In scrapbooking, the choice of adhesive is particularly important, because certain glues lose their binding ability after many years and leave behind a sticky residue that may permanently damage photos and other keepsakes.

What's the right acid-free adhesive for you? That's easy—experiment until you find the one you like to use.

- *Double-stick tapes are a good option for photos, since they lie down smoothly under various scrapbook materials.*

- *Two-way glue gives you great flexibility. Squeeze out just a bit, let it dry, and temporarily position items for a "post-it note" effect; squeeze out more and put the item in place right away while it's still wet for a permanent bond. A standard brand is SIG two-way glue.*

- *VP glue is a pH neutral glue that has been used for years by bookbinders and other artists. VP, or polyvinyl acetate, is a white glue that dries clear and forms a long-lasting bond.*

Glue sticks are best used for adhering large keepsakes to your pages, because they can be messy when used with smaller items like photos. Some glue sticks may not be permanent, so call the product's customer service department if you are in doubt about its qualities.

Mounting corners provide an old-fashioned, classic look. These little black triangular paper corners were once the only option for securing pictures in scrapbooks. If you have heritage photos you don't want to damage, mounting corners give you the option of removing them when you wish. Most corners, now available in many colors, including clear, are self adhesive or can be affixed with the archival adhesive you choose. You can even make your own by cutting small triangles from acid-free paper.

The Goody Bag

Besides album, paper, glue, and scissors, what else can help you get started? The following materials create good organization . . . and could even generate sparks of creativity.

Page protectors keep photographs on facing pages from touching and safeguard pages in three-ring binders from dust and handling. Protectors are made of clear plastic. (See Keeping It Safe on page 36 for information about archival plastics.)

If you plan to use newspaper clippings or other high-acid items in your scrapbooks, deacidification spray will help protect the surrounding materials. You can buy this spray through archival mail order suppliers.

When you get your photos back from developing, do you wonder if aliens have invaded your pictures? The ever-present "red eye" is a problem that can be eliminated with some special cameras. For an easy way to touch up existing pictures, use a red-eye pen, which filters out the red glow.

Common manila envelopes are handy for sorting and storing photographs and materials by theme or category. However, if you think it may be years before you get your photos into an album, invest in archival envelopes. (See Resource Section on page 239 for suppliers.)

If you're part of the information age, software and special computer scrapbook programs can help combine video clips, pictures, stories, audio clips, layouts, die-cut shapes, fonts, and clip art graphics all on one page. You can enjoy a "virtual" scrapbook stored safely in your computer or print it out for a more tactile experience. A variety of programs, compact disks, and floppy disks are available at computer stores, in scrapbooking stores and on the Internet.

Hearts and Flowers

You'll find store shelves sagging under the many thousands of newly popular decorative items on the market for scrapbooks. Indulge to your heart's content. These materials, which can all be found in craft, art supply, and discount stores, include:

- *Stickers, available in many sizes, colors, and motifs, add instant spot color, whimsy, and spice to a page, especially when used in moderation.*

- *Die cuts, available in many sizes and colors, are cut from varied weights of paper to add a thematic shape to a scrapbook page. They are*

sold individually or in theme packets.

- *Paper punches cut accent paper or cardstock into small shapes to decorate a page. They are available in many sizes and motifs, including stars, hearts, butterflies, and bears.*

- *Corner rounders, similar to paper punches, trim square corners into curved corners.*

- *Templates are used to trim photographs and papers into shapes, such as circles, ovals, and hearts. You can also use cookie cutters as templates.*

- *Rubber stamps, used with pigment ink pads or brush markers, add colorful accents to a scrapbook page. They are available in almost any motif imaginable. Color Box and Cat's Eye are two companies that make archival ink pads.*

Marvin Davis is a former advertising agency president who now runs Romancing the Woods out of his home in Woodstock, New York. Dedicated to the lost art of garden and woodland architectural structures in the picturesque style of 19th century European estate parks and Adirondack Great Camps, the company has done work for many of the Hudson Valley's historical sites and has been featured in the New York Times.

Marvin's scrapbooks reflect his personal passions: cooking and travel. Searching out the origins of regional foods, eating with the local people, and absorbing all the color and flavors of a region can be best kept alive by daily scribbling in a travel diary or scrapbook. Like this one from a trip to Venice, his albums combine photographs, both intact and cut-out, sketches, journalizing, bills of fare, restaurant menus, maps, and anything else that catches his fancy. Notice his use of cut-out photographs of gondolas interspersed with sketches of the boats, the well-planned layout, and the "panoramic" view from the hotel room made up of three separate shots.

PART TWO: MAKE A SCRAPBOOK

I have more memories than if I were a thousand years old.

— Charles Baudelaire

You've sorted through hundreds of photographs, negatives, old letters, ticket stubs, autographs. You've picked out your favorite scrapbook album, papers, and glue. You've got a spot where you can work. It's time to begin.

Start with the very next roll of film you bring home from the drug store or the camera shop. Sort through those pictures, right then and there, and pick out the best shots. Be ruthless about tossing out-of-focus, over- or underexposed shots or the stray photo of a complete stranger's big toe—unlike wine, such photos won't get any better with age. While your thoughts are still fresh, jot down important information about each picture (or batch of pictures) you decide to keep. Store your notes with your pictures; when you're ready to write descriptions in your scrapbook, they'll be handy. (See more about *Journal Writing* on page 65.)

Keep these pictures in chronological order, in envelopes or photo sleeves, until you sort them into separate photo boxes, by theme or by person. Don't forget to organize and label your negatives as well at this time—it takes just a few minutes, and it can save you hours later.

Just by going through a few simple steps every time you bring home pictures, you'll have a head start on the scrapbooking game. Remember the old adage, "A journey of a thousand miles begins with a single step"? You've just taken your first sure steps on the scrapbooking road.

We learn to do something by doing it. There is no other way.

— John Holt, educator

Dive Right In

It's loads of fun to tap into your creativity with scrapbooking, but keep in mind the important thing—get the stories and photos in the book. Your first pages may seem a little plain, but you will still feel satisfied that you've captured the information. Don't get caught up in being perfect—you'll waste time while memories go unrecorded.

Here's how Scrapbook Guild member Marie Nuccitelli remembers getting started on her very first page:

"I bought the basic supplies for an 8 1/2" x 11" album (cardstock, binder, adhesives, pen, scissors, page protectors) and borrowed some punches, fancy scissors, and a couple of templates. Then I looked through the first pictures we took of our newborn daughter. When I decided which pictures I wanted on the first page, I started cropping. Then I added them to the cardstock, put a few stickers on, wrote a couple of things, and put the finished page in a protector."

Sound simple? It is.

Layout Design

As you try to decide which pictures and other materials to put on a page, remember that you're looking for a design that will have an emotional impact—a way to make people feel the same things you feel about your theme. To help accomplish that, focus on a favorite or most important photo, then build the page around it. Whether you add a few other pictures, a fetching border, or a catchy verse of poetry, with a strong central photo you know your foundation is solid.

Just as you chose a theme for your overall scrapbook, each page can have its own theme, like a subplot in a novel. Grouping pictures together that have something in common creates this effect. You could bunch photos around one special event, outdoor summer fun, or a few favorite toys. Each theme page might call for a particular color scheme or graphic style, like using warm earthy colors for a gardening page or flowery script for a Valentine's Day page.

The layout sets the tone and mood for the theme. For instance, if you have a group of sports photos with lots of action, a layout with lots of angles will make the movement feel as if it extends onto the whole page. Baby pictures and wedding pictures usually call for a softer, quieter layout.

In general, depending on your album size and paper size, start with two to four photos for each page. This gives you a starting point. Try a few, add a few, subtract a couple. Get a feel for what looks best to you. Remember, you want the page to look interesting, but not too crowded.

An attractive layout has a comfortable flow for the eye to follow. The photos and other elements, like journal writing, decoration, and memorabilia, complement each other. They have a relationship to one another and a definite order of importance according to size and placement.

We learn to read from left to right and top to bottom, so our eyes are already trained to look at a page in that way. You can use this to your advantage and draw attention to your liveliest, largest, or most interesting photo by placing it on the top left-hand corner of the page. Another natural attraction for our eyes is to look at the outside edges of a page. Your mind often combines the aesthetic nature of a page's edge and the learned aspects of reading. By placing your most interesting photo in the top right corner of a right-hand page or the left corner of the left-hand page, your eyes are automatically drawn to your important photo. The eye will then naturally shift back and down and around, creating an "S" movement on the page. Keeping this natural eye movement in mind can help you place photos to their best advantage.

You can put your main photo on a pedestal by using what designers call the "law of opposites." Place the main photo on a different angle than the other photos; the main photo could be horizontal with the surrounding pictures on an angle or vice versa. Or crop the best photo in a different shape from the other pictures. Try placing your favorite photo slightly off-center in the top one-third of the page for extra interest.

Simplicity is bliss, or so they say. Using too many elements to express your theme—diecuts, stamps, stickers, too many colors—can confuse the viewer and distract from the main subject of the photographs. For dramatic effect, often one special picture with a handmade border is perfect.

You may want a scrapbook that is consistent throughout, with not much variation in the style of each page. Choosing compatible papers, colors, and decorations helps to achieve this. To maintain the overall theme, but add interest to the composition in other ways, crop and place photos and text in unexpected ways.

As you plan your page, remember some pictures will need description, so map out a space for the words as well. Some pages may also need a title and decoration, such as a border or photo mat.

If you have difficulty with a page and feel stuck, you may need a new perspective. Try different colors or textures of background paper. Sometimes a new color combination will help things come together in a bright new way. If the page is still not working, reevaluate your theme. If you're not completely comfortable with your theme, lose it and find another. You need a theme that can keep you excited about your page.

For more layout inspiration, look through *Scrapbook Ideas* on page 97. Also try magazine and newspaper advertisements, cereal boxes, a favorite coffee table book, even your high school yearbook—anything that has a lively, interesting layout.

Rose Gonnella (Scrapbook Guild) makes a habit of buying a few extra stamps whenever she goes to the post office. Not a true collector—she isn't particularly interested in the rare or valuable—she searches for the visually arresting stamp. Depending on the size of an individual stamp, Rose designs an artful composition for her scrapbook with one or two or many stamps on each spread. The small album is of her own handicraft as well; she makes her own paper and binds the book.

Layout is a skill that you will improve with practice. Meanwhile, don't be overwhelmed. Just think of the joy the finished page of "your" life will bring down the years. That perspective usually gives your creative spirits a lift.

Cropping

How do you cut photos, drawings, certificates, and other mementos to fit together in your scrapbook? By cropping, which is the art of "sculpting" two-dimensional items with scissors, a craft knife, or a paper cutter. Cropping, or cutting, a photograph can emphasize a person's face, get rid of an unwanted background, or change the standard rectangle into a fun, fascinating shape.

First of all—and this is fundamentally important—make SURE you want to cut the photo. You can't uncut what scissors or knives have taken asunder. Just like a carpenter with a board, measure twice, cut once. Or in this case, consider twice. If you don't have

a duplicate or the negative, photocopy the photo. Or have a duplicate or negative made before you cut. Then crop the copy or duplicate without anxiety.

Some pictures may have a distracting background or other people you do not want to include on a particular page. For these pictures, cutting away everything but the main subject may give you an unusual shape you need for a page. For example, an egg shape for Easter or a snowflake for a winter birthday.

See-through templates, available in ovals, hearts, circles, and many other unusual shapes, offer an easy way to crop out unwanted backgrounds. At least take a look—you might find inspiration. (See a free-form handcut shape in the *Best Friends Scrapbook* on page 103.)

Think twice before cropping out all of the background. Sometimes things we take for granted, like the new little maple tree in the front yard or the beat-up old Tercel in the driveway, may tell viewers years from now more about the passage of time than that brand new haircut.

For straight-edge cropping, use a metal ruler as the edge to follow and a very sharp-bladed craft knife to cut. Place a sheet of paper on top of the photo before cropping to protect it from fingerprints. A mini paper cutter also works well for neatly cutting straight edges on photos.

Journal Writing

A picture may sometimes be worth a thousand words . . . but not when it comes to scrapbooks. Journal writing transforms a picture album into a storybook with bits of written information, in small doses. Consider the alternative: have you ever come across a batch of old family pictures that have no information? It can be so frustrating. The picture raises lots more questions than it answers. Who are these people? What are they doing? Is that little boy Granddaddy? Why is everyone dressed up like that? What year was this anyway?

Keep these basic kinds of questions in mind as you begin documenting your photographs. It might help to remember the five Ws of Journalism 101—Who, What, When, Where, Why. No matter how beautiful your page of photos may be, or how cute the new diecut, the story's not complete until the words connect with your design. The premise is that your words will be there to tell the story, even when you are not. Like a good novel, your scrapbook will transport those who look inside into new, wonderful, and comfortably familiar worlds. (See journal writing and lettering samples in *Scrapbook Ideas* on page 97.)

It's not a scientific report, so be as subjective as you want. Add your own personal feelings and impressions of an event or person. Stretch your imagination. You could include favorite songs, television shows, computer games, movies, poetry, magazines, and books that relate to the photographs or people pictured. It's your scrapbook.

There are some essentials when it comes to describing the photos in your book. You want to record the full names of the individuals, plus the date, the place and some information about what is going on in the photo. Be as thorough as you can while you still remember the details of the photo. You don't have to be stuffy about recording the information. For instance, a family nickname is usually fine, but make sure the person's full name is used at least once in a scrapbook. Future family members may never have heard of Sugar Foot or The Professor.

When working on a genealogical album, you might find information from older living relatives of tremendous value. (See *Genealogical/Family Archives Scrapbook* on Page 143.) Here's a tip. Before you interview your relative, prepare a list of questions in advance. Weed out or rephrase questions that elicit a simple yes or no answer—you want responses that in themselves tell you something about the relative. A terrific book to use as an interviewing resource is *To Our Children's Children: Preserving Family Histories for Generations to Come,* by Bob Greene and D.G. Fulford (Doubleday, 1993). If your note-taking skills are a little rusty, consider taking along a tape recorder or video camera. Make sure equipment is in good working order before you begin. (Mainly, this means check the batteries.)

Writer's Block

For many scrapbookers, it's fear of their own handwriting that keeps them from recording their memories. What if I make a mistake? What if the writing is crooked? What if I misspell something? If your handwriting gives you writer's block, there are several ways to help get you unstuck.

First, take a deep breath and try to slow

down. Visualize a beautifully written, completed journal. Just relaxing can improve your handwriting immensely.

Next, try taking the time to pencil in your thoughts on a separate page. Knowing that it's not permanent, that you can make changes, will free you to write the information you need. If you want an extra bit of guidance on the "real" page, use a metal ruler as a straight edge and follow the line. You can use a pencil here to write your thoughts, then ink over the top of the penciled words when you get them just right. When it's the way you want it—and the ink is completely dry—you can erase the pencil marks. This technique is best used on sturdy paper and with very light pencil markings.

Lettering booklets give samples and how-to information about different writing styles, such as dot, block, or outline lettering. A little practice can make you a master. A calligraphy pen adds a real touch of class. (See *Write This Way, Please* on page 50 for descriptions of other writing instruments.) Computer type can also be printed out onto archival paper with a high resolution printer. Cut letters or phrases to the appropriate size, then glue in your book.

But remember that your own handwriting, even if it looks like chicken scratches to you, could be the most treasured piece of your scrapbook in generations to come. Just think how much you love seeing your own grandmother's graceful handwriting today! Perhaps what makes individual handwriting so important to loved ones is what you have to say. If it's legible, it's wonderful. Handwriting says something about character, and it says a lot about love, too.

Memorabilia

Words and pictures tell a memorable, if partial, story on the pages of your scrapbook. For the whole story, sometimes, it takes a bit more—a pressed violet from your grandmother's garden, your son's baby bracelet from the hospital, a wedding announcement printed in your hometown newspaper. The memorabilia of our lives comes in many shapes, sizes, and textures. While variety surely is a spice of life, assortments of materials can mean trouble for the longevity of your scrapbook. (See *Keeping It Safe* on page 36 for more about archival concerns.)

It is very important to keep your mementos and memorabilia separate from the photographs in your scrapbook. Methods of doing this vary, but here are the basics.

Newspaper clippings and other types of lesser-quality paper documents, like ticket stubs and government papers, possess high acidity. This creates the problem of acid migration, a condition that occurs when the acid bleeds out into nearby paper. Keeping newspaper clippings and photos apart can be done in several ways. You can put clippings together on pages without photos. Or you can place them in protective mylar sleeves. One of the safest ways to save newspaper clippings is simply to photocopy them onto acid-free paper. You can also use a deacidification spray on newspaper articles and other high-acid paper items.

Another choice is encapsulation, which seals the page on the edges only. Two sheets of mylar make the container of choice with this method. Archival containers also protect documents by keeping them safe from sunlight, dust, and excessive handling. Lamination may seem like another great solution. After all, it seems to keep everything safely sealed up. Resist this temptation! The combination of the heat process and the adhesives that bind the plastic can cause irreversible damage.

For odd-sized mementos, you can find mylar and acid-free plastic packets from many scrapbook supply stores. (See *Resource Section* for archival suppliers.) Some packets have several different sized trays on a hole-punched sheet; others have just a single window that attaches to a page. You may have items that need a uniquely shaped pocket . . . or a pocket of unusual size. You can even make the holders you need for such mementos yourself, with archival paper. (See the recipe pocket in the *Cook's Scrapbook* on page 119.) Some items can be stitched onto the page as well—needless to say, consider what might be on the other side of the page. You wouldn't want extra stitches in Aunt Irene!

Use acid-free and lignin-free paper to buffer the photos. Acid from mementos will migrate to the paper rather than to the precious photos in the rest of your scrapbook.

To feature extra-special mementos, use an entire page for a single item. That really gives it distinction and a place of honor. (See the *Collector's Scrapbook* on page 115.) Old letters or documents should be open and flat, not folded. The fold causes a lot of stress on the paper, and it will eventually crack. You'd hate to lose the most romantic line of Grandpa's proposal to Grandma.

For larger mementos that you want to include in your scrapbook, take a photo of the item. Then make a special page including the photo and journal writing about the importance of the item. You can store the actual memento in an archival box.

Scrapbook Makeover

Photo albums or scrapbooks you put together many years ago or perhaps inherited from your great aunt Elizabeth may hold treasures that are looking a bit worse for the wear. Yellowed, brittle, and faded photos stare out from every page. Birth and wedding announcements, stuck down with school glue and clear tape, have nearly turned to dust. Photos kept in magnetic photo albums look quite foggy and will not budge. Or, maybe only last year you made a new scrapbook. Not having read this book yet, you plastered photos and letters all over non-archival pages, using scotch tape and even staples.

It's time for a scrapbook makeover.

The condition of a scrapbook really warrants a good hard look before you tackle the delicate work of a makeover. You will need to decide whether it's best to dismantle the album and bring it up to archival standards or store it safely as is, and not risk any damage that handling and rearranging might cause.

If your album is crumbling beyond repair, first consider removing only the most important photos and items and putting them into a new archival album. It can be quite difficult to remove old photos because of the different adhesives that may have been used. Since tearing is always a possibility, consider copying the pictures before you attempt to remove them, just in case.

In some instances, the information in the album is just as important as the photos themselves. The life of such albums can be prolonged by placing acid-free tissue between the pages, then putting the entire album in an archival box. This will slow the inevitable effects of light, dust, and excessive handling. (See *Resource Section* on page 239 for archival products.) You'll add years, and maybe even decades, to the album's life.

Many of your favorite pictures might be encased in magnetic page photo albums, popular for their apparent convenience. Their plastic pages are very acidic, which spells disaster in the end for your precious memories. If the photos have begun to bond with the adhesive in the album it may be tricky to remove them. Be as gentle as possible while sliding a butter knife or cake spatula between the photo and the album page. Keep your patience at all times. If you cannot remove them, and if you can't locate the negatives, you can have them color copied. Place the copies in an acid-free album for posterity.

Usually photos that were long ago taped into a scrapbook will have long since fallen out or at least become detached from the page, but occasionally, taped pictures seem stuck for good. In this case, try using a blow dryer on the back of the page to remove the pictures. The heat will loosen the adhesive on the tape. Be careful not to overexpose the photo to the heat.

If tearing does occur while taking your oldest scrapbooks apart, or if some of the photos are already torn, many photo shops specialize in restoring and retouching old photos by hand or by computer. Such a shop can make you feel as restored as your newly touched-up photo.

Finding the Time

To choose time is to save time.

— Francis Bacon

Set aside an evening once a week or twice a month to sort old photos and mementos. As you get your materials organized, schedule time regularly just for scrapbooking. If you put only four pages in a book per month, you could have a book, maybe two, finished in less than a year. Set easy-to-reach goals like this so you can record your progress.

Do you have kids who turn into little jealous tornadoes whenever you sit down with a project? Let them play along beside you . . . as they work on their own scrapbooks. Or wait until the children are asleep, then work uninterrupted for even a few minutes each night.

Many scrapbookers gather together regularly at "crops" to work on their scrapbooks and share supplies and ideas. This can be a marvelous opportunity to get a fresh outlook on layout, organization, and catchy themes from fellow scrapbookers. (See the *Scrapbook Socials* section on page 223 for more about the boundless scrapbook community.)

Make time to scrapbook. There's no other way to make it happen.

*M*arie Nuccitelli *(Scrapbook Guild) has kept track of everything in her children's lives by making scrapbooks. From birthdays and holidays to hospital stays and dentist's visits, she's there with her scissors and glue. In these two pages, Marie combines decorative edges made with paper edging scissors, hand-drawn patterns, printed information about her son's unusual name, and handwritten captions to describe her daughter's Fourth of July contest.*

PARTTHREE: TIPS
AND
TECHNIQUES

. . . in black ink my love may still shine bright.

— from Sonnet LXV,
William Shakespeare

In this section, Scrapbook Guild members, who've been sorting and cropping for years, offer firsthand advice to keep you going strong.

Getting Started

Stick to it. If you spend even a few hours a week at first, it'll be more hours than you've spent in the past. The results will show in no time. When you're consistent and block out time every week for scrapbooking, your book takes form almost magically.

Where to start? Build your first page from a current batch of photos. Then work backwards, organizing and sorting through older photos and mementos. By working with images freshly stamped in your mind, the process will go faster and you'll be less likely to feel overwhelmed. Your own progress will become all the encouragement you need.

Work Space

Organize, organize, organize. Keep your work space organized. It makes the time you spend scrapbooking more productive and more enjoyable . . . and you'll rarely find yourself on hands and knees in a closet searching for a lost glue stick.

Books on wheels. If space is limited, keep your supplies organized in a transportable system, such as drawers on rollers that are available at office supply stores. This way, you can put your supplies away in the closet, then roll them out to the kitchen table or another convenient location when you find a chance to work.

"I have a pretty ideal work-space: an eight-foot table with a hutch; two shelves in the closet next to my table; a computer and printer on the other end of the table; and all my supplies neatly organized in the

hutch and on the shelves. I also have a file cabinet under the table to hold my various cardstock and decorative paper, along with my scrap paper (my class materials are also stored in this file cabinet). And for projects in progress, I have stacked paper trays to organize different albums. This is all in a room that is off on the side of our apartment, and I can leave things where they lay if I am interrupted. We also have a phone in the room, so I can even talk to someone while I'm scrapbooking!"

— Marie Nuccitelli,
Scrapbook Guild

Make It Yourself

Become a sponge. Consider taking a bookbinding or hand-papermaking course at a local art center or college. Course materials—and being around other people—will expand your creative potential for scrapbooking.

Valentines at your fingertips. Make your own stencils by cutting out shapes you trace from cookie cutters, coloring books, or any books filled with simple objects. Cut the shape out of cardboard or disposable plastic lids.

"When you make the album yourself you can control all of the variables. You will be able to choose the appropriate paper, determine page size, decide on the number of pages, and be able to adapt your scrapbook for any particular purpose."

— Jody Williams,
Scrapbook Guild

Make your own stickers. Apply double-edged photo tape to the edge of your choice of paper, then punch out the design with a paper punch. When you peel the backing off the tape, you have a homemade sticker—in just the right design, color, and style.

Pocket protectors. To make a pocket page to hold memorabilia, such as letters, cards, or newspaper clippings, you need two sheets of archival paper, some scissors, and glue. Cut a curve from the top of one sheet of paper, then glue the two sheets together down the sides and across the bottom. Leave the top open—you can easily slip in mementos . . . and slip them out again.

Buying and Storing Supplies

Take one, please. When you buy a new type of product that you've never used, buy only one. It's tempting to buy every cute rubber stamp on the shelf, but try your favorite first. You can see immediately if it's really useful for you.

Bulk up. Once you know your needs, buy acid-free, lignin-free cardstock in bulk at a local stationery store or business supply discount store. Small packages purchased at specialty stores will run up the cost of your project.

Say cheese. Buy film in bulk too. (More than six rolls is usually considered bulk.) Don't go hog wild, though—film can expire. Check expiration dates carefully before you spend your money.

> *"Go to a class or a workshop to try out new supplies and gadgets. Or ask a friend to borrow some before you buy them for yourself. If you buy only the materials you need for the next few pages or for the one season you are working on, you don't have so much to store. Pick and choose wisely, and you won't be discouraged later by feeling that you've somehow 'wasted' money or time on scrapbooking."*
>
> — Jennia Hart,
> Scrapbook Guild

Check the Internet. At various "swap sites," you can exchange supplies you no longer use for something you need or something new you want to try. (See page 242 for some suggested web sites.)

Zip it up. Plastic zipper bags are very useful for storing small supplies, like stickers or scraps. With larger bags, you can even organize bulky supplies, like paper punches or rubber stamps. If you really want to be efficient, punch holes in one side of zipper bags, then store them in three-ring binders, sorted by color or occasion.

Stick around. Sort stickers by theme and store them in baseball-card holders or page protectors with pockets of varying sizes. You can easily store your stickers in a three-ring binder, once you've corralled them.

File, don't pile. Organize 8" x 10" paper by color and theme in hanging files in a file cabinet. Or place them in page protectors inside a three-ring binder. It will save you the frustration of digging through mounds of material for the color you want.

A box cantata. Scissors, large rubber stamps, colored markers, and the like can be stored in clear plastic boxes. Then you can stack these conveniently out of the way. It keeps things neat . . . and you can still see what's inside each box.

Penny Prince Delany is an artist, illustrator, and children's book author. She specializes in nature themes and has a botanical illustration degree from the New York Botanical Garden. A drawing teacher, she founded the DRAW (Develop the Raw Ability Within) program, a course for children and adults she gives in Irvington-on-Hudson, New York. She lives there with her husband, an investment banker and a nephew of the Delany sisters of book and Broadway fame, and their four children.

She never leaves home without her scrapbooks, which she has filled with pencil and pen and ink sketches and notes on various flora she observes. These books then serve as a reference from which to create more polished artwork. Note that she always dates the page, describes colors and texture in words as well as images, and keeps track of how long the sketch took her.

Have a cigar . . . box. Store stickers flat, dry, and away from light. A cigar box or an expandable file works perfectly for this.

Stamp out clutter. If you have enough rubber stamps to line your living room walls, here's an organizing suggestion. On a single piece of paper, make an impression of the design on each of your stamps. Then use this master the way you would an index—you can see everything you have at a glance . . . instead of looking at every rubber stamp for the dozenth time.

And cut out clutter. Use the same idea for paper punches. One sheet holding every pattern of all your punches makes it easy to see what you have.

And wipe out clutter. Do you have a baby—or a grandbaby—in diapers? Hang on to empty baby-wipe containers. Label the outside, then use to store paper punches, scissors, or glue.

Neat as a pen. To prolong the life of your pens, store them horizontally. That way, the tip doesn't dry out as quickly.

"Once you have sorted and labeled and are ready to get going, keep up the habit. Each time you develop a new roll of film, put it in the right place as soon as you get home. Once you have found a system for organizing your supplies, be sure to put away any new supplies you collect. If you stay organized, you will find you have more time to enjoy sorting your photos and other memorabilia."

— Marie Nuccitelli

Dedicated to the craft you love. Try to keep all your supplies organized and in one place that you devote to scrapbooking. You'll find it easier to switch into your imaginative gear . . . and scrapbook supplies won't get mixed up with other craft projects you may be working on.

Organization

Plain manila. At the beginning of a calendar or school year, label manila folders with the names of each family member. Create another folder for extended family members and the family as a whole. File school papers, cards, documents, and other items in this way and they'll already be sorted when it's time to use them in your scrapbooks.

Stand up straight. Try to store documents, certificates, letters, and other materials in a vertical position. If you stack items, they rub against each other. Over weeks and months, this can damage them.

Storing Photos and Negatives

Touch me nots! During long-term storage, negatives, like photos, should not be allowed to touch each other. It's easy for negatives to scratch one another, despite their smooth appearance.

"I usually leave my photos in the developer's envelope, filed by date. I sort the photos I will use immediately in a scrapbook into sheet protectors. Eventually, I hope to put all the double prints into photo sleeves just as they are — no cropping or anything, except names and dates written with a photo pen or pencil on the back. I leave the photos in the developer's envelopes only until I put them on pages or into sleeves. I store all my negatives in negative sleeves I have purchased and then file them."

— Marie Nuccitelli

Storing Scrapbooks

Be careful! Handle scrapbooks with care so that you do not tear pages, break bindings, or tear contents loose.

> *"Scrapbooks are beautiful works of art and should be kept out on a special table or gathered with other albums and placed in an open basket or decorative box. When they're in plain view, everyone can touch, see, and enjoy them."*
>
> — Rose Gonnella,
> Scrapbook Guild

Warps and all. Store small- and medium-sized scrapbooks on bookshelves—vertically!—between similarly sized books. This will minimize warping, which can be a definite problem in humid climates, like those in the Deep South states.

Safe beneath the covers. Tie with flat cotton or linen tape any scrapbooks that have loose or detached covers. Tie the knot at the side of the album to prevent indentations on the cover. If your scrapbook is older and damaged, try wrapping it loosely in acid-free paper, then tying it with the flat tape.

Flat-earth society. Store scrapbooks flat if they contain heavier objects, such as pamphlets, maps, or documents.

Stay cool. Try to keep the temperature and humidity where you store your scrapbooks as constant as possible. The ideal? Try 70 degrees with a humidity level of 50 percent.

Theme

Follow your bliss. When choosing your first scrapbook theme, decide on your great interest. If you are more involved with a child than the garden club, you will probably have more enthusiasm for a child-focused book. Enthusiasm is the spark that makes creativity catch fire and burn bright.

Time isn't everything. If you create themed scrapbooks instead of books that simply cover events from one time to another, it should be much easier to get started. A strong theme gives you a framework to build on. Chronology is fine, but you might find it less inspiring.

"It's best to wade through the materials you have and sort them by year, activity, or person. Look it all over after the sorting and see if a theme reveals itself. Scrapbooks don't have to cover enormous periods of time or be only about milestone events. You can make a little scrapbook concerning one evening at the theater with a friend or an afternoon hiking trip. I spent four days in Rome with my cousin, Thomas. I photographed him in front of walls that were various shades of orange. I put these photos and other memorabilia into a book and gave it to him. He adores it."

— Rose Gonnella

Group dynamics. Group photos according to subject—outdoor play, eating, bedtime—in separate envelopes. When you have enough pictures in that subject, you'll have a theme page ready.

Design

Stamp it out! When you use rubber stamps, first press an image on plain acid-free paper or cardstock. Then glue the stamped paper onto your finished page. This way, if you make a mistake—or don't like the results—you'll only have to throw away a small piece of paper, not a whole scrapbook page.

Or . . . If you make a mistake on a page, don't throw it away. Instead cut out a sheet of complementary paper, then use it to cover the mistake. You might be surprised by the new look you've created. That's what we call scrapbooking serendipity.

"I treat every page in a scrapbook as a small collage. When it's time to build a page, I begin with one strong image and use it as the central motif to determine other choices. Rummaging through my files, I find backgrounds, borders, other accent images to layer together. I like to combine textures, such as a rumpled paper sack smoothed out and used as background behind an elegant cutout print of fine china. Then I might sew a fancy embroidery stitch border around the layers by hand."

— Charlotte Lyons

Frame and glory. Save the frames from purchased diecuts. They can serve as templates you can use to trace shapes onto paper. They can also be used as a photo mat. The frame can even be used as scrap paper for small paper punches.

All the marbles. Wrapping paper, marbleized paper, and other handmade papers can be glued into the inside front and back covers of your scrapbook. (Take note: these may not be archival papers, so use your judgment.) The bright, unique pages make the books very personal.

"I always crop photos. Not only does it allow me to eliminate unwanted areas, it also keeps the scrapbook from becoming monotonous, by varying the shape and dimensions of the photos."

— Jody Williams

Energy by design. Use colors and shapes that help portray your theme. Bright colors and defined angles introduce an energetic theme, for example, while subtle pastels and rounded, smoother shapes build formal or quieter themes.

To the net. Check the Internet for tons of page layout ideas. (See page 242 for web site addresses.)

"If you have a one-of-a-kind photo, don't crop it. Get a reprint or copy made, or better yet, use the negative. If you still want to use the original photo after that, lay the picture down on your page and cut a mat to frame the photo in the way that you want to crop it. This gives you the freedom to shape the photo without having to cut it."

— Marie Nuccitelli

Photocropping

Leave Miss Marple some clues. Be careful to leave visible details that identify people, dates, or occasions in your photos. A spanking new yellow Mustang in which the family sits smiling, plainly says "1968." The Nikes on little Charlie's feet tell us it's the 1990s.

"I save almost everything. Some people may think I'm a bit obsessive, but I like to think I'm just sentimental. What an eclectic collection my grandchildren will get to sift through!"

— Patricia Dreame Wilson, Scrapbook Guild

Don't cut Polaroids! Do not crop an instant photo (like a Polaroid). Cropping releases processing chemicals from inside the image, which destroys the picture. If the white frame bothers you, just make a mat that covers it.

Memorabilia

Things to save. Collect newspaper clippings, certificates, ticket stubs, souvenir programs, brochures, letters, postage stamps, hospital bracelets, leaves, flowers, Scout badges, announcements, autographs, children's drawings, locks of hair, marriage licenses, ribbons, engraved napkins, maps, etc. Your life is a living museum for your scrapbook.

Become a copycat. You probably have precious documents, small three-dimensional objects, or other items that need to be kept elsewhere instead of being glued to scrapbook pages. You can still scrapbook them! Simply make color photocopies to use in your work.

Play the accordion. Accordion files are great for organizing, sorting and storing cards, letters, and other treasures. Label the files by year or by person, then add any other pertinent information.

Careful with the clippers. When you cut clippings from a newspaper or magazine, leave extra space at the bottom, top, and sides. This way, you can fold the extra paper over and glue it to your album page.

No blind dates. Try to leave the title and the date of the publication visible when you cut out a clipping so you can identify it later.

A stitch in time. Place bulky items—dried flowers or political buttons, for example—in polyethylene zipper bags. You can then stitch them to your page with cotton thread.

"I keep a small blank journal in the kitchen, one in my office, one in the car, and one by my bed. That way I always have one nearby so I can jot down the next amazing thing my four-year-old daughter says before I forget it."

— Patricia Dreame Wilson

Constructive criticism. School work and art projects give true personality to a child's scrapbook. Often, however, the materials are very acidic—construction paper is a notorious culprit. Either keep these treasures in a separate binder or make photocopies on acid-free paper or cardstock.

The Words

Put it in writing. Always write in your scrapbooks. If you're not the type who has much to say, then just say a few words, but always write something. It's the kind of personal touch that will be loved by future generations.

Words as design element. If you don't have enough pictures for a page, fill it in with your own words. Too much decoration can be cluttering, but the words add information, emotion, and a different graphic element to a page.

Two heads are better. Give extra thought to what you want to say about a group of pictures. Talk it over with someone else if you need to. A good conversation always helps make sense of an abstract idea.

Our daily bread. Write down your thoughts and experiences in a daily journal, or whenever you can. Use this journal as a source when scrapbooking.

Write with a flourish. Try a handwriting or calligraphy class. You'll have fun and learn a beautiful new skill to use in your scrapbooks.

Clip more than coupons. Trace and transfer clip-art graphics to your scrapbook for an added decorative effect. A Victorian or Celtic initial letter, for example, can enliven a page with a historic mood.

Record the facts. Always include names and dates on the backs of pictures with a photo pen. If one sad day, photographs separate from your page, you'll still have the details that help you place them back where they belong. (See page 50 for suggested pens.)

Put someone's words in your own mouth. If you can't find your own words to describe a photo, use someone else's. Look for a poem, song lyrics, a common saying—even a greeting card message. Anything works if it says what you feel. (See page 240 for suggested sources for quotations.)

"Be cautious about the 'industry labels' that will lead you to believe the products out there are what you need. Learn the lingo, and then make your own informed choices about how archival you want to be when putting your scrapbooks together. Some people are happy cutting their photos, using papers with some lignin in them, or using markers that are 'safe,' but not permanent. Others would rather not take any chances."

— Marie Nuccitelli

Acid-Free or not?

Cleanliness is next to . . . Always wash your hands before handling photos or working in your scrapbook. Natural oils in your skin can react with photographs or paper in unusual ways. It's a simple thing, but cleanliness really protects your album.

Negative capability. All photos have a natural life cycle; you can't expect them to last forever. Negatives will retain the image much longer than a print, so take good care of them.

Reprints charming. Color negatives have a shorter life than black and white negatives. After 15 or 20 years, a color negative will not reproduce perfectly, even though you'll get some sort of an image. For extra safety, you may want to have reprints made every ten years or so.

Expert care. Photo and camera shops can restore most damaged photos. To repair a historical photo, however, contact a conservator who specializes in archival photos. How do you find a conservator where you live? Write or call the American Institute for Conservation of Historic and Artistic Works (see page 248 for contact information).

Let the buyer beware! Many mail-order catalogs and department stores sell beautiful-looking scrapbook albums. Always ask before buying if the product is archival, then decide if you still want it.

Vacation Tips

Exciting new people and places bring out the shutterbug in most of us. Any time you have lots of photos a scrapbook can't be far behind. Here are some tips on capturing vacation memories from Scrapbook Guild member Jennia Hart:

Create memory flashcards. Cut up acid-free, lignin-free white paper into 3" x 5" cards. (Look for this reasonably priced paper at a stationery store.) Take these cards along, and jot down events, stories, dates, notes, captions, and the names of people and places. When

you get home, use the cards as a reference. Or mat them and include them in your album.

An instant album. Purchase a small spiral-bound album for you and your children to use as a journal for vacation memories on the road. Use a pencil to "x" out several pages, then go back and add a few photos to these pages after you get home. Voila! An instant album.

Precious memories. Document your trip every night after the kids are in bed. Write down those memorable happenings before the details slip away.

Kid stuff. Give the kids a small camera. They can take photos of you, their favorite vacation spots, their cousins, the inside of your ear . . . whatever strikes their fancy. Their personal perspective and memories of the family vacation will be recorded for the family album too.

Buspersons holiday. If you are on a long vacation, you might take your supplies and work on your pages at night in your motel room . . . or even in your tent. It's been done!

Bag your memories. Save all vacation memorabilia in large plastic zipper bags. Take one bag for each day of your trip and place in it everything you want to save. At the end of the day, date the bag.

"Scrapbooks don't have to be large. Try a book about five inches square. It forces you to crop photos and pick out the best parts of things. I love tiny scrapbooks commemorating beautiful little things in life."

— Rose Gonnella

Caught mapping. Don't forget to save the maps, too. A traced map makes a great title page. A map treated with deacidification spray can also be used as a part of your album.

Tell us about the 1960s, Grandma Chris . . . If you are visiting relatives and you're anxious to learn more about family history, be sure to take a list of questions to ask them. You will learn more from a few well-phrased questions than if you just say, "Tell me about your life."

And finally . . .

Space . . . the final frontier. Leave at least the first and last pages of a scrapbook blank for added protection against handling.

Ink in a blink. If you don't have ink pads in every color under the sun, brush-tip pens work double-duty as a quick way to ink rubber stamps.

Dates are great. Remember to put the date on your scrapbooks, not just on the pictures inside them. This tells the whole story of when the photos were taken and when the scrapbook was compiled.

Extra care with photos. When labeling and dating photos, write on the back edge, not in the middle of the picture. This is an extra precaution—it protects the picture even when you use a photo-safe pen.

Enjoy the Process

A new scrapbooker from Canada, Maureen Guretzki, said her two-year-old son, Joey, just loves to look through his scrapbook. All their relatives live hours away, but right in his own bedroom, anytime he wants, he can see "Gampa" on his "tactor."

Like this tyke, we are drawn to the simple art of scrapbooking for personal reasons. The most compelling is our love of family. Scrapbooks unite us with friends and family in distant places, even those who are long departed. Scrapbooks bring the past to life. In so doing, they bring life to the present.

"Don't be too worried about perfection. Remember to enjoy what you are doing and try not to compete with another wonderful page that you have seen. Don't think you have to have a page worthy of publication in a magazine. If you have an idea that you want to try, try it! If you like a style of page you have done before, keep doing that same style. Just work on your pages in a way that is most satisfying to you."

— Marie Nuccitelli

In the hubbub of buying supplies, sorting through photos, and tracking down answers to who, what, when, where, and why, remember your mission. Who are you putting the scrapbook together for? Why? Most of all, remember to have fun.

Chef and author Jacques Pépin and his wife, Gloria, live in Madison, Connecticut, where he is able to indulge his creative ability in the form of paintings and mosaics. Further evidence of his artistic skill is to be found in the unique scrapbooks he has kept for many years. He documents every dinner party with watercolors, pen and ink drawings, handwritten menus, often in French, wine labels, and signatures and comments from his guests. To date, he has six scrapbooks filled to the brim with mementos of memorable meals.

6 juillet 91
ADVENTURES UNLIMITED

Le menu
A WINTZENHEIM HAUT-RHIN FRANCE

En Apéritif *Pommery* 1981
De Venoges 1977
Une
Madison —

Assiette de Poissons fumés Pepin
ALSACE
TOKAY PINOT GRIS *Vieille Vignes* **1987**
VIEILLE VIGNE
Zind Humbrecht

Côte de Veau grillée
Le Tour Haut Brion 1970
* Château Larcombes 1965

Porte Fromages
Domaine Zind Humbrecht

Vosne-Romanée La Grande Rue Lamarche 1985
Clos de la Roche DUJAC 1972

Compote de Fruits
Château de FARGUES 1966

POMMERY

POMMERY

LOVE

A great evening
to share fine
wines with
fine people

Bali & Lewis

A wonderful evening...

PARTFOUR:

THIRTY SCRAPBOOK IDEAS

How vast a memory has Love!

— Alexander Pope

ANNIVERSARIES
SCRAPBOOK

A formal collage graces the title page of an anniversaries scrapbook.

A party, dinner, a live performance, or a cruise are the traditional ways of celebrating the anniversary of many milestones. Scrapbooking extends an anniversary by providing an enduring spot for memories.

Besides the obvious weddings and births, there are "hidden" moments that may be earmarked for celebration. The anniversary of a big move from California to New York could prompt an annual family dinner to review changes and toast successful transitions. Anniversaries of special achievements such as citizenship, graduate school graduation, the last payment on a mortgage, or the number of years in a particular company may be noted with a luncheon, bouquet of flowers, or bottle of champagne.

For your anniversaries scrapbook, think about including:

- *A list of all the anniversary celebrations and gifts.*

- *Cards and letters from family, friends, and acquaintances.*

- *Wine labels, pressed flowers, ribbons, and wrapping from gifts.*

- *Any printed material related to the event such as papers registered at the founding of a business, club bylaws, wedding license, or letter of offer of employment.*

- *Photographs taken during celebrations.*

- *Ticket stubs from a performance, travel itineraries, or menus from the restaurants where you got together for an anniversary.*

Greeting cards, ribbons, etc., are mounted in a group. If you want access to the various layers, mount the cards with photo tabs so they can be lifted off the page. At right, a photo enlargement embellished with a Victorian-style paper frame.

- *Photographs that relate to the reason for an anniversary.*

- *Quotes, song lyrics, and/or poems from each year you celebrate.*

- *A newspaper masthead recording the date of each anniversary. If you didn't remember to save a newspaper from your wedding day or other event, call the publisher and ask if you can order one. Usually, copies are available in print or on film for a nominal fee.*

Have you let years of anniversaries pass without saving cards, wine labels, ticket stubs, or

HAPPY ALL THE TIME
—Laurie Colwin

LEAVE A KISS WITH MY
CUP AND I WILL
NOT ASK FOR
WINE
—Alice walker

Graphic organization using a modular grid system. These four-page spreads commemorate two separate anniversary celebrations within one scrapbook. Each spread repeats a specific sequence thus bringing organization to a variety of images and printed materials.

other memorabilia? Don't dismay. A scrapbook does not have to be complete before you start. Scrapbooking begins with a desire to honor memories, not a photograph or greeting card. You probably saved more than you recall. Look through your files, bookshelves, boxes of photographs (what do you know, that's where you stashed that concert ticket from Woodstock!), dresser drawers, basement, attic, garage, and your parents' closets. There are probably a few items waiting to be rescued from obscurity and mounted in a scrapbook.

To preserve and display your photographs and other materials, a three-ring (sometimes called O-Ring) scrapbook with cloth covers is an excellent choice. It provides elegance and flexibility. Look for pages that are heavy-weight polypropylene and insert paper that is acid- and lignin-free. This type of scrapbook holds approximately 50 pages. Colors usually come in black or off-white— try using both! The contrasting color pages can face each other and distinguish between photographs and printed materials such as letters and postcards. Sleeves and paper inserts can be purchased conveniently in separate packages of ten.

Although an anniversary scrapbook will most likely be chronological, you can create a logical visual sequence as well. Magazine, newspaper, and book designers use modular design systems called "grids," to create a logical visual sequence for readers. Survey all your materials and determine a simple modular system, e.g. the first entry in the system is a single photograph with a date and anecdote, the second page is a collage of greeting cards faced by a page of six photographs; the ending page contains an appropriate literary quote. You repeat your module for each anniversary date throughout the scrapbook. A modular system results in an easy to follow design and a visual arrangement that assists in distinguishing each celebration.

The first page of your anniversary scrapbook can include a title, date, and a representative photograph from the commemorated event.

BEST FRIENDS
SCRAPBOOK

Your road will be made
smooth for you by good friends.

*A fortune cookie slip below a photo-booth picture of two
best friends makes a nice cover.*

A scrapbook celebrating friendships can

commemorate a few unique moments or

document an expanse of years.

To start your scrapbook, gather all your

photos and other items. Look over the

contents and decide on how to arrange it.

A chronological order is one possibility

but you might divide your scrapbook into

sections based on specific shared

experiences. For instance, all the places

you visited followed by a list of the music and books that you enjoyed together, which then leads to related items.

General friendship scrapbook pages might contain:

- *Letters, postcards, and notes you've exchanged—use whole or cut-out portions that matter most.*

- *Recipes shared, along with anecdotes about their use and success.*

- *Tags and ribbons from gifts you've given to each other. Too lovely to throw away, so why not save for a scrapbook entry?*

- *Pressed flowers or plants from a walk you took together, a bridesmaid bouquet, or simply symbolic. Ivy, for instance, is emblematic of friendship.*

- *Packaging from your favorite things such as candy wrappers, luxurious lotions or bubble bath, sneakers, cigar labels, seed packs, lipstick.*

- *Fortunes from all those Chinese dinners you've*

Combine the ribbons and wrapping from gifts with hand-lettered anecdotal information and the handwriting of your best friend for a warm personal memory.

had together: Your road will be made smooth for you by good friends.

- *Wine labels from special occasions.*

- *Meaningful quotes from poems or song lyrics chosen specifically for the scrapbook.*

Make a collage of cards, letters, and other mementos on a single page. Or color photocopy the items and cut them up for a layout while preserving the originals in a side envelope.

- *A postcard reproduction from an art exhibit. (Didn't you wait on line for an hour in the pouring rain to see the once-in-a-lifetime Vermeer show at the National Gallery?)*

- *Ticket stubs from theater, sporting, or other events you attended together.*

- *Travel itineraries along with addresses, schedules, and other information on the trip—then you could repeat a special vacation exactly the way you arranged it the first time.*

- *Of course, all sorts of photographs. If possible, include one of the place where your friendship started and each of your current homes. You can edit photos by cropping to focus on the elements most important to scrapbook.*

Expandable binders allow memories to grow and grow. But if you want the scrapbook to be a keepsake about a specific time or you choose to give the scrapbook as a gift, then a permanent binding is better. You could even create your own binding, which allows you to choose the exact paper for each page. Some hand–binding techniques are simple and deeply rewarding. What better gift for your best friend than a book you bound yourself?

It adds a personal touch to have samples of your friend's handwriting in a best friends scrapbook. Once you've almost finished it, you can ask your friend to add written comments to caption photographs and memorabilia.

For the cover, a photocopy enlargement of a letter or postcard works well. For decorative effects, hand-color with colored pencils or artist's crayons. Another idea is to make a cover titled with your two names. Or, instead of lettering, a framed photograph of two best friends can say it all.

Print up or handwrite a list of favorite things shared within a friendship. Then trim it with decorative edging and arrange with a photograph.

BOOKS WE LOVE

Ethan Frome
Wuthering Heights
The Maple Stories
Like Water for Chocolate
Time and Again

BIRTHDAY GIFT SCRAPBOOK

Friends and family celebrate a 40th birthday.

This scrapbook for an adult's birthday involves other people's participation. First, you will need to solicit help from friends, relatives, former teachers, coaches, employers, teammates, and anyone else you can think of. One woman mailed the following request to about 50 of her husband's friends and relatives:

Dear Friends and Family:

My beloved husband Jon is turning 40 this summer. More than anything, he'd like to invite you to his birthday party. But we realize you might not be able to make it. So I'd like to surprise him with a special album filled with messages from all of you. Would you please send me a letter, photograph, or other memento that signifies something about your relationship to Jon? It might be a description of a shared experience, a funny story, your first impression of him, a photograph of yourself either alone or with Jon, an object small enough to fit in a scrapbook, or anything else you can think of.

A chain reaction resulted, in which one person led her to other long-lost acquaintances, so that in the end she had letters, telegrams, e-mail, faxes, cards, photographs, newspaper clippings, and original drawings from almost 100 people. In this case, she arranged them randomly in a standard, oversized photo album with heavy black paper pages. You could, however, try to put the scrapbook in order by chronology, geography, or even according to how close to each person the birthday recipient was or is.

Capture the birthday girl in a "happy" mood and blow up the image to a full 10" x 14" inches. She will love seeing herself in such close-up detail. Don't forget to include words of encouragement and support.

Along with letters, cards, and mementos, you can also include:

- *(40) photographs of the recipient from birth to the present.*

- *Biographical information.*

- *Business cards for every job the person has held or a list of job titles.*

- *Copies of identification cards including driver's license, social security card, birth certificate,*

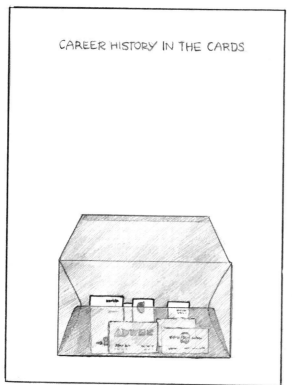

CAREER HISTORY IN THE CARDS

CHARTING JON'S LIFE

FAMILY HAPPINESS

WORK

OTHER

FRIENDS

Recording the biography of the birthday person is a wonderful compliment. At left, a translucent vellum envelope glued to the page holds business cards from various jobs. At right, a "pie-chart" of photographs creates a visual biographical overview.

passport, library card, or business tags.

- *Photographs of family, friends, and acquaintances at significant moments.*

- *Photographs of the childhood home, school, college, and the workplace.*

- *Photographs of significant moments such as a first time driving a car or graduation day.*

- *A copy of any educational diploma, letters of recommendation, or report cards from kindergarten through graduate school.*

- *Memorabilia the recipient saved: medals, road race numbers, airline tickets, invitations, buttons from the person's own political or humorous collection, matchbooks, ticket stubs from significant events the person has attended. For example, a rock concert he went to on the first date he ever had with his future wife—you'll have to sneak it out of the shoe box from under his side of the bed. Also, check the glove compartment of his car and his golf bag (if you dare) to find other treasures for the scrapbook.*

- *Articles published about the person.*

- *Receipts for large, special items like a red sports car.*

- *Artwork: cartoons, illustrations, photocopies of paintings or portraits.*

Since this scrapbook is a gift, a beautiful handmade leather binder is worth splurging on. Many custom bookbinders can add gold stamped or blind-embossed lettering to the cover for a perfectly elegant title. It will certainly impress the recipient. See page 245 of *Resource* section to order handmade and personalized leather books and binders.

As for layout, try to balance the number of photographs with other media when arranging the composition of your birthday gift scrapbook. A limited number of images highlight important moments while keeping the chronological flow easy to follow and the viewer on track.

CHILD'S BIRTHDAY SCRAPBOOK

A simple sewn binding and a child's drawing of her own birthday cake for a truly sweet scrapbook cover.

Happy Birthday to me! What day of the year is more important to children than their own day, lovingly planned and joyfully celebrated with a heaping frosted cake, gifts, and games. Like the vertical ruler measuring height on the doorway of a child's bedroom, a birthday scrapbook is a pictorial growth chart. Start a birthday scrapbook with the actual day of birth! Include a copy of the birth certificate and/or a copy of an adoption record. Also, incorporate notes from the birth event or adoption proceedings.

Pages of a child's birthday scrapbook include:

- *Photographs of each birthday party or birthday outing.*

- *Photographs of family and friends celebrating.*

- *Invitations, cards, and thank-you notes.*

- *Anecdotes on gifts received. Get your child involved in the commentating.*

- *Wrapping paper remnants.*

- *Party favors or napkins that record the party's theme.*

When composing your scrapbook pages, don't feel stuck with the 4" x 6" snapshot format. You can trim your photos for optimal compositions. Crop the photograph of the child blowing out the candles of the cake so only the child is visible. This makes the child's peak moment the entire focus. The photo can be used as it is or brought to a color copier and enlarged to fill one whole page of the scrapbook.

Marina's Sixth Birthday

She chose to have a
Victorian tea party celebration

Fancy borders and scalloped edging are charming.

Mount photographs of family and friends on pages in a collage—cutting to create interesting shapes that fit together like a puzzle. Or, you can cut your photos with decorative edges using specialized scissors for this pur-

A birthday scrapbook is a good place for creative play. On the left page, the printed number four is repeated many times over to form a decorative pattern. At right, a cut-out photo with mylar confetti on several layers of colorful paper.

pose. Let the decorative edging reflect the gleeful party atmosphere.

With a party mood in mind, you can sprinkle some of the scrapbook pages with confetti—avoid the crepe-paper type for these won't glue well. Try little shapes made of colored mylar. You can buy stars, hearts, rocking horses, and teddy bears among other playful cutouts.

Commercial, decorative paper or—even better—handmade frames surrounding photos add a celebratory mood to the scrapbook. Be aware that these frames can be overbearing. Try a limited use of frames to keep the photos from being crowded by ornamentation.

Take advantage of each birthday being a different number by printing out from a computer a large size numeral to mark the scrapbook page. Don't rely on the computer itself for effects. Use the printed version and trace it onto colorful paper, then cut it out. Or, print on to a heavy paper (as heavy as recommended for

your particular printer) and paint with acrylics over the numeral to give it texture and color.

Record specifics about your child's height, weight, and other physical statistics at each age. Also record his or her likes and dislikes—favorite food, book, movie. You'll be amazed by what changes and what stays the same.

A child's birthday scrapbook deserves a festive cover. Glue mylar confetti around decorative computer lettering of the name of the child. Letters cut out of colorful paper are also fun. Or invite the child to draw a picture of a birthday cake and make this the cover or first page of the scrapbook.

COLLECTOR'S SCRAPBOOK

A traditional Japanese sewn binding for a stamp collector's scrapbook. Actual stamps are adhered with archival glue.

Whether long established or recently begun, grand or humble, meticulous or casual, a personal collection of any sort is enhanced and shared through a scrapbook. For resolute collectors, a scrapbook might highlight one aspect of their collection e.g., all the ancient Roman coins from a larger world coin collection. Along with a description and photo of the coins and proud collector, there might be accompanying purchase information such as receipts, catalog materials, date of acquisition, and personal anecdotes. A collector's scrapbook might point out just the unique or the unusual pieces in an overarching collection. If the collecting is on a small scale, then the collection in its entirety can be made into a scrapbook. You can use all the wine labels from bottles consumed at special dinners with friends or all the beautiful contemporary stamps you've collected and enjoyed for their aesthetic value.

An expanded wine label scrapbook might include:

- *Photos of the wine country and/or friends at dinner.*

- *The wine list.*

- *Notes on where you bought each wine.*

- *Anecdotes or history about the vintner.*

- *Notes on the vintage.*

- *Quotes from authors, chefs, or your uncle in the wine business describing the heavenly creation distilled from grapes.*

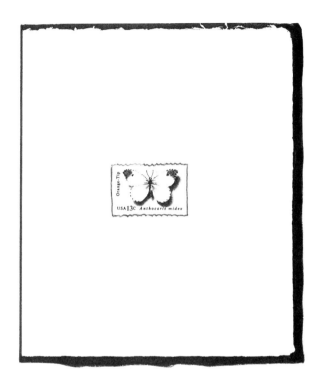

To raise your cherished collection onto a "scrapbook pedestal," mount each item one to a page. The scrapbook itself is bound by sewing together sheets of handmade paper. The deckle edges of the paper have a soft, natural quality.

A single stamp scrapbook could include:

- *Postcards or postmarked envelopes bearing the collected stamp.*

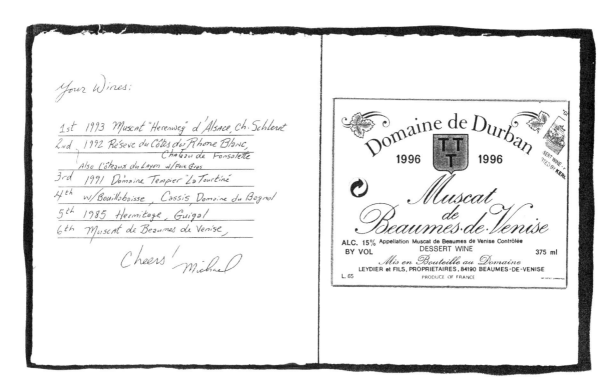

Your Wines:

1st 1993 Muscat "Herenweg" d'Alsace, Ch. Schlerat
2nd 1992 Réseve du Côtes du Rhone Blanc,
            Chateau de Fonsalette
   Also L'ôteaux du Layon w/Foie Gras
3rd 1991 Domaine Tempier "La Tourtiné"
4th w/Bouillabaisse, Cassis, Domaine du Bagnol
5th 1985 Hermitage, Guigal
6th Muscat de Beaumes de Venise,

        Cheers! Michael

An annotated two-page spread from a wine lover's scrapbook. The label slides off the bottle after soaking in warm water for several hours. Dry between sheets of wax paper and adhere to your scrapbook page with archival glue. Use a wide sponge brush to spread glue evenly.

- *A record of the first date of issue and its distribution.*

- *Any special information on the stamp such as awards it received or whether it marked a change in denomination for U.S. postage fees.*

- *Notes on the stamp's artist and how he created the image: watercolor, engraving, paint.*

- *Information on the subject of the stamp; for instance, the accomplishments of the person depicted on the stamp or a history of the selection process. (How did Elvis rate a stamp?)*

- *Autographs with a photo of the famous person on the facing page.*

- *Ephemera collections (cigar boxes, packaging, theater programs).*

- *Matchbook collection.*

- *Postcard collection.*

One tip for scrapbooking a collection is to keep the object one to a page whether it is a stamp, a wine label, baseball card, or a photocopy of an antique coin. By isolating an item on the right page and writing anecdotes on the left facing page, the object can be viewed clearly and appreciated in itself. One to a page, the collected item is placed on a "scrapbook pedestal."

Other collections that work well one to a page:

A hand-bound book made with simple sewing techniques allows you to pick the exact number of pages as well as the paper used for interior pages and the cover.

You might buy a sheet of beautiful handmade paper and use it as the cover without any further embellishment. Or, the scrapbook cover can be one item centered on the front. Another idea is to have all of the contents pictured in a neat grid on the cover. Photos or actual labels, stamps, etc. can be photocopied in color, cut up, and reassembled into a free-form pattern or orderly composition.

COOK'S SCRAPBOOK

A handmade scrapbook does not have to be difficult to make. This is a traditional Japanese sewn binding.

When cooking becomes a full-fledged hobby, the triumphs of the kitchen can be preserved (no pun intended) in a scrapbook containing memories of marvelous food, wine, meals, and friends. Using the following ideas, you can organize your scrapbook as a remembrance of all good things.

Scrapbook pages might include:

- *Your most successful and/or favorite recipes: either your own or from others.*

- *Photographs of the cook and assistants or guests in the kitchen, at a meal, or on an outing.*

- *Cooking tips from family and friends: Aunt Jennie's surefire way of puffing pastry, Lisa's best method for making chocolate curls, Frank's carving techniques.*

- *A list of tips from professional chefs.*

- *Autographs of well-known chefs.*

- *Quotes from literature on the glories of food: "Small cheer and great welcome make a merry feast." —William Shakespeare.*

- *Menus written in calligraphy, illustrated with simple clip art or drawings.*

- *Labels from jars and boxes of favorite ingredients such as vinegars, chutneys, cocoa, pasta, and wine.*

- *Dried and pressed herbs and flowers.*

- *Documentation on purchases of special cooking equipment.*

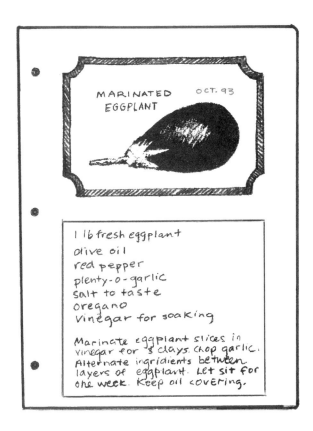

MARINATED EGGPLANT   OCT. 93

1 lb fresh eggplant
olive oil
red pepper
plenty-o-garlic
salt to taste
oregano
vinegar for soaking

Marinate eggplant slices in vinegar for 3 days. chop garlic. Alternate ingridients between layers of eggplant. Let sit for one week. Keep oil covering.

Handmade labels and handwritten recipes bring a home-spun quality to your scrapbook pages.

- *Newspaper and magazine clippings. Wouldn't late novelist and essayist Laurie Colwin's charming article "Desserts that Quiver" be worth saving?*

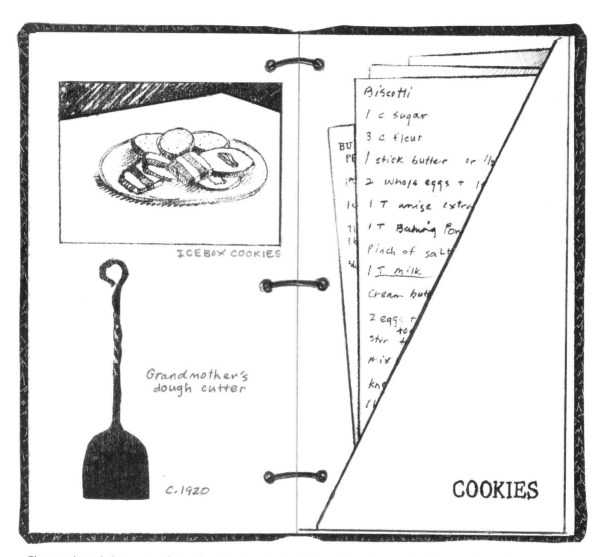

ICEBOX COOKIES

Grandmother's
dough cutter

C. 1920

Biscotti

1 c sugar

3 c flour

1 stick butter   or 1/2

2 whole eggs + 1

1 T anise extra

1 T Baking Pow

Pinch of salt

1 T milk

Cream butt

2 eggs +
    to
Stir t

mix

kne

(l

BU
PE

COOKIES

Photographs and photocopies of utensils add color and visual information to the text. Envelopes can be punched with holes to fit into a ring binder. Loose items placed in the envelope can be easily removed for kitchen use.

- *An address section for where to buy hard-to-find ingredients.*

- *Photographs of table settings.*

- *Invitations to dinner parties and a record of the guests.*

- *Menus from your most lauded dinner parties, printed on a computer in a special font. (Hint: try Desdemona.)*

- *Old recipe cards in your mother's or grandmother's original handwriting.*

- *Notes from cooking classes.*

- *Award certificates and ribbons. These don't need to be formal. Include the thank-you drawing your nephew sent you of the luscious strawberry shortcake you made for him.*

You can bind your cook's scrapbook in a number of ways. Try a single expanding book of sturdy blank pages in which mementos are fixed. Or use a combination binding of blank pages and pocket folders. Glue items and photographs to pages and keep recipes, lists, and other two-sided or large items in the folders. A handy feature of using folders is that you can remove recipes when you cook without risking soiling the scrapbook.

Photocopied color enlargements of paintings or photographs adhered to the outside of a plain album make a wonderful cover for your cook's scrapbook—perhaps a reproduction of a beautiful 18th century Dutch still life of food. You can create an orderly collage of food paintings from many different artists, or use an enlargement of a great recipe, especially if it is handwritten with lots of comments and asides. The most simple cover is a paper-framed photograph of the cook in his kitchen.

You can always cook up a more specialized theme scrapbook—bread making, baker's scrapbook, exotic foods. Or try one of the following:

- *An Heirloom Recipe scrapbook.*

- *Jams, Jellies, and Preserves scrapbook.*

FAMILY REUNION SCRAPBOOK

Signatures surround the family photograph to make an informative and decorative title page.

A family reunion takes a bit of effort to organize. As long as you're choosing the date, time, place, food, etc., add plans for a scrapbook as well. With a little advance preparation, a family reunion scrapbook can go far beyond a few photographs to become a valuable and cherished family record.

Before the reunion send everyone a copy of "things to do for the reunion" with a friendly request to post the list on the refrigerator:

- Ask each family member for an inexpensive, passport-like (usually less than two inches) photograph to put in the scrapbook. Ask each person to find a meaningful quote, gleaned from a philosopher, spiritual leader, poem, song lyric, prose, newspaper, or fairy tale (adults can help children or kids can list their favorite book title). Each family member will have one scrapbook page with a photo, quote, or small memorabilia.

- Depending on the size of your family you can group small individual photos on one or two pages with the name and birth date of the person below.

- Have everyone bring one picture of their last vacation for the scrapbook.

- Encourage family members to bring a photocopy or photograph of any important documents to share, such as marriage or birth certificates, diplomas, letters from far-flung relatives, medals of honor, or a family heirloom.

During the reunion:

- Have each family member sign the scrapbook. Go a step further—add a thumb print, a hand print, or a special drawing.

A decorative piece of printed paper, appropriate to the season, fills the left page and complements the small photo at right. A caption is placed directly below the image.

- Organize a group photo. Give everyone something whimsical to wear—a goofy hat or a funny nose and glasses.

- Gather all the cousins who look alike and photograph them together.

- Take photographs at the beginning, middle, and end of the reunion (everyone waving good-bye). Arrange them in sequence in your scrapbook.

1959
Family Reunion
at our ancestral home
Nantucket, Massachusetts,
1659

At left, a photo enlargement of a family group fills the page. At right, the family crest and an elegant caption created with a formal script typeface.

Other possible scrapbook pages could include:

- *The invitation to the reunion.*

- *A list of the food, and who baked, broiled, or burned which dishes.*

- *A list of family milestones and achievements.*

- *An address section and/or birth date section.*

- *A photo or drawing of the great-grandparents' homestead.*

- *Any new information to add to the family genealogy.*

Funny sunglasses competition at the annual family reunion.

After the reunion, gather all your content and photos and divide them into related groups. The book can be a chronology of the day or pages might be grouped according to each nuclear family.

The big group photograph of all family members makes a great cover. Place the photo at the center bottom of the album with a printed title at the top. You could use family members' signatures for the cover of your reunion scrapbook. If the handwritten names are too large to fit, then either reduce the signatures on a photocopy machine or print them on a computer instead. If the names are written on thin paper you should adhere a stronger backing to it before gluing it to the cover.

If this is a jointly created but one-of-a-kind scrapbook, the rights to ownership might become problematic. Rather than risk a family squabble over the treasure, try passing the book around from year to year so it rotates its position in the family. Or have a lottery—the winner becomes the designated guardian.

FIELD GUIDE SCRAPBOOK

Accordion fold binder made with paper embedded with leaves, grasses, and flower petals.

The last few pages of a commercial field guide are often left blank for readers to record the place and date of a specific sighting of bird or plant. There is never enough space for more than a few brief words. A field guide scrapbook allows for a more complete and engaging record of the flora and fauna a person or group has researched, discovered, and observed.

Pages of a field guide scrapbook could include:

- *Photocopies of birds, fish, plants, etc., from the commercial field guides, accompanied by your own sighting information.*

- *Your own field sketches and photographs of animal tracks, vistas, unusual specimens.*

- *In-depth information about the creatures that were observed. Plenty of space is available in a scrapbook to discuss any curious features of the sighting or particular circumstances of the day.*

- *Seasonal list of field information such as all the birds sighted during the autumn at a favorite reserve.*

- *Scientific anecdotes gleaned from supplementary reading.*

- *Personal milestones such as the time you finally tracked down a Glaucous gull to complete your sightings of all the seagulls of the Northeast.*

- *Photographs and notes on particular outings or special trips to hunt the wild . . . whatever.*

GIANT PUFFBALL

Fruiting body large, globular, smooth, growing directly from ground; white when young, dingy later. Where found: rich disturbed soil; open places, barnyards, pastures. Warning: make sure the interior flesh is pure white; bitter when yellowish. Cut open to be certain there is no rudimentary stem or gills.

Close-up photography showing an edible puffball mushroom. On left facing page, field notes typed and mounted for a clean look.

- *Brochures from parks and wildlife reserves.*

- *Ticket stubs and notes from wildlife lectures you attend.*

- *Endangered species list.*

- *Pressed leaves, grass, petals, or feathers.*

- *Record of involvement with environmental activism (so you can remember which senators were pro-conservation).*

- *Quotes from naturalists, scientists, and environmentalists you admire.*

SITED:
VERMONT
JULY 97

Resting in low ground cover, nest seems to be made of moss. The bright orange yellow feather caught my eye first as a sweet and tiny thing. with a tralce. L'gurally warble but also don't get close... a sharp sound, quarolacsdup will erup...

CANADIAN WARBLER

red
bright yellow
field notes
← Pink legs
Blue Grey upper feathers
white undertail coverts

→ WARBLER EATS INSECTS BUT THIS WAS A NICE BERRY SAMPLE, SO I DREW IT TOO.

Sketches, handwritten field notes, and a photograph arranged on several pages to record a bird siting with both freshness and accuracy.

Organize your field guide scrapbook relative to the flora and fauna observed or compose by season, location, or both. Think of a scrapbook on winter birdwatching, local mushrooms, seashells, or spring flowers in the Northwest. Your scrapbook can have a casual flow based on a random list of favorite wildlife, or a more formal structure perhaps organized in alphabetical or chronological order.

Cover or title page designs can be hand lettered, printed words, or you can choose to use a photograph by itself. Type and image together is more of a challenge to compose. One hint for success is to keep the design as simple as possible. When in doubt, edit out.

An elegant, textured cover without text or images is always an option as well. Beautiful, custom handmade paper, embedded with wisps of grass or leaves, suggests the natural subject matter of the scrapbook. Other custom papers have printed patterns of birds or flowers. Both types of papers can be ordered from Aiko's Art Materials Import (see page 247 in *Resource Section*) or found at better art supply stores.

FIRST TIMES SCRAPBOOK

The
Very Special
1st
T I M E

By using a variety of sizes and styles of letters (italics, bold, all capitals) on the cover, you place importance on specific words.

For parents, a child's "first time" event is cause for a miniature celebration. The first time a child walks, visits a dentist, or gets a haircut can be photographed, recorded, and collected into a loving scrapbook.

You might have recorded some first time experiences already. By using the ideas below you can plan your child's first times scrapbook now:

- *First time walking and first word—photograph the moment, and jot down date, time and place, and the word!*

- First haircut—before and after photograph with the haircutter; a business card from the salon; a lock of hair; a record of the conversation between the child and the haircutter.

- First dentist visit—a photograph in the dentist chair with the office staff; any certificate or little prizes given by the dentist.

- First day of school—photographs at home, on the way, and outside the school; registration letters; bus schedule.

- First bike ride and/or the first time on a two-wheeler—beside a photo, try copying the manufacturer's lettering on the bike using tracing paper and transferring it to a scrapbook page.

- First time swimming, diving, skiing, fishing, catching a ball—photograph the event and save any printed material or receipts.

- First team sport—photos with the team and individual photos, any certificate or registration materials.

- First time on public transportation—save the bus or train ticket stubs, include a map of destination.

FIRST TIME
ON SANTA'S LAP

(it was a little scary)

A first time might be a tearful occasion. But the scary moment can be turned into a special memory by adding a heartwarming decorative border and some sympathetic captions. Use stickers, stamps, or printed paper.

- First vacation—if it was a mountain camping vacation, try pressing and saving a tree leaf or fern and including it along with photos, maps,

FIRST
TEAM SPORT

A star player

Patterns are wonderful for attracting attention and decorating a page. Use rubber stamps to make your own patterns. Printed papers work fine too. Enlarge one unit of the pattern to frame your photograph and add some handwritten captions for a personal touch.

and other memorabilia. If it was a beach vacation, take a photo of a sand castle along with photocopies of seashells and the little red plastic shovel that helped to build the castle. The advantage of a photocopy is that it inexpensively reproduces at actual size or enlargement; any three-dimensional objects can be placed on a photocopier.

- First graduation—awards, any cards, certificates, diplomas (or copies), or other printed materials can be included along with formal and casual photographs of the event.

First times never really stop happening. It is up to you to decide when to stop. Keeping that in mind, the binding for a first times scrapbook should be expandable. Choose a book that allows for additional pages and purchase a supply of extras for future use.

You'll want an appropriate cover or title page for your child's first times scrapbook. A cover image could reflect the theme of the book:

- An oversized number one or lots of little number ones cut out from magazines or greeting cards.

- Enlarge a photograph of your child's hand forming the number one with his/her finger.

- An oversized image of a clock with the hands pointing to the number one.

- Create an overall pattern out of the number one using a homemade stamp and a colorful ink stamp pad.

MARY'S FIRST SNOWMAN

WITH HAT, MITTENS AND A NEW SUIT

DECEMBER 30 1 9 9 6

FISHING SCRAPBOOK

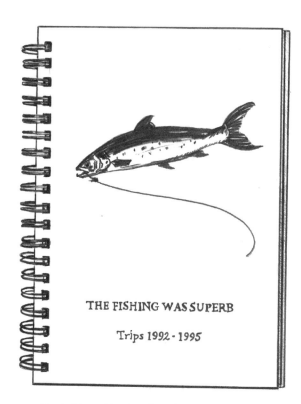

THE FISHING WAS SUPERB

Trips 1992 - 1995

A spiral-bound book with a plain paper cover is perfect for a fishing scrapbook. Draw, paint, or glue images and type directly onto the cover.

Anyone who frequently looks through a tackle box with a sigh and smile, or who keeps ratty old fishing equipment for sentimental reasons, deserves a scrapbook. Creating a scrapbook for a fisherman is also a good way to show respect and encouragement for this contemplative sport.

Some scrapbook pages might include:

- *Almanac or newspaper clippings on tides and times, and weather.*

- *Photographs of the big fish that did not get away.*

- *Stories about the ones that did get away . . .*

oops, the ones that were thrown back in the water.

- Photos of the fisher folk in action.

- A list of great fishing spots and the fish caught there.

- Photos of those favorite beaches, streams, lakes, or rivers.

- Anatomical drawings of fish and comical illustrations of fish "personalities."

- A list of all the various types of fish that have been caught and where.

- Photos or drawings of the fisherman's favorite lures with anecdotal information about the lure.

- Receipts from fishing equipment purchases.

- Photos of a day at the tackle shop.

- Photo and autograph of the person who showed the fisherman how to tie his first fly.

- A bumper sticker that reads: "A bad day at fishing is better than a good day at work."

- Names of boats owned or rented.

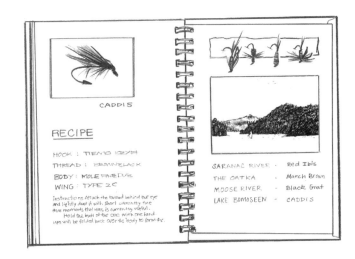

Actual flies are hooked into a strip of archival tape. Handwritten information accompanies photographs of fishing spots and a close-up view of a favorite hand-tied fly.

- A list of clever or beautiful names on other boats: Sea Again, Mandalay, Fi-na-lee, Pier Pressure, Always Off Shore, Record Breaker, Gimme-a-Break.

- Fishing derby entry certificates and awards.

- Quotes by famous fishermen and/or passages from literature about fishing; see Ernest Hemingway's Old Man and the Sea, Herman

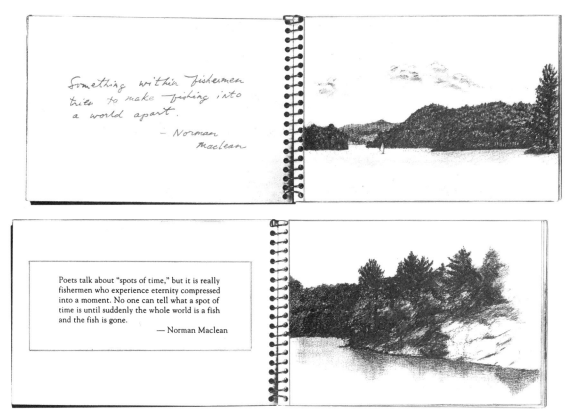

Something within fishermen
tries to make fishing into
a world apart.
— Norman
Maclean

Poets talk about "spots of time," but it is really
fishermen who experience eternity compressed
into a moment. No one can tell what a spot of
time is until suddenly the whole world is a fish
and the fish is gone.
— Norman Maclean

Two examples using quotes to caption your photographs. At the top, handwriting creates a personal feeling; below, printed type is more formal.

Melville's Moby-Dick, *or Norman Maclean's* A River Runs Through It.

You might organize the scrapbook in categories such as sections on the fish, on the fisherman, on equipment, and other miscellaneous information and photos. Of course, the scrapbook could also be chronological or a simple free-flowing stream of memorabilia and photos that record the many pleasures of fishing.

An expandable album works well or a binding with big rings (reminiscent of the rings on a fishing pole) is appropriate. Suggesting the color of water, a blue or blue-green covering for the scrapbook certainly is inviting.

GARDENING SCRAPBOOK

For the cover or title of your gardening scrapbook, crop the actual or photocopied seed packet and add home-grown lettering.

Whether you have a formal garden on several acres or a few modest beds of perennials and herbs, a garden scrapbook is a great way to extend your gardening "season." Scrapbooking can lead beyond simple record keeping into an expansive personal journal that documents garden plans, seed and plant resources, favorite blooms, philosophical thoughts, planting triumphs, and happy mishaps—after you gave a basket of zucchinis to everyone you knew, what did you do with the 50 baskets that were left?

To grow a garden scrapbook, try:

- *Drawings of your garden scheme.*

- *Photographs of your garden and other gardens you've visited. A camera with a macro lens allows for detailed close-up shots of your flowers.*

- *Extend the joy of beautiful cut flower bouquets with a photograph to place in your scrapbook.*

- *Photographs clipped from magazines and garden catalogs.*

- *Tips and techniques from gardening friends and professionals.*

- *Pressed flowers or leaves.*

- *Articles and bits of advice clipped from newspapers, magazines, and brochures.*

- *Seed packages with your own notes.*

- *A list of seed companies and nurseries that have been most helpful.*

- *An account of your seasonal plantings to record successes and less-than-successful growth.*

- *A bibliography of gardening books. With this list available, you don't have to tax your mem-*

SEPTEMBER BOUQUET
- - - - - - - - - - - - - - - -

I went to the bookstore this morning. On my arrival home, I stopped in the garden to pick some straw flowers for a bouquet. I popped the blooms into my shopping bag so I could tote them indoors. The golden September flowers looked so pretty in the little brown sack that I decided to make a vase out of the bag. Straw flowers need no water, so the fit was delightfully serendipitous.

Combine your personal gardening stories with a silhouette image of representative flowers, plants, or veggies for a gardening journal.

ory each time you return to the library to borrow a book for a second time.

- *Printed materials from any botanical gardens you've visited.*

- *Botanical drawings you've sketched or reproductions from books and postcards.*

- *A list of garden stores and catalog resources with their addresses and phone numbers.*

A seasonal arrangement would be a logical

Keep rosemary by your garden gate.

Add pepper to your mashed potatoes.

Plant roses and lavender, for luck.

Fall in love whenever you can.

— Alice Hoffman

A gardening scrapbook can be romantic. On the right page, a photo enlargement of roses. The image dramatically fills the whole page and is accompanied by a charming literary quote on a facing page. The curved type was created in a drawing program on a computer. If drawing software is not available, ask the technicians at your local quick-print shop for help. They can follow your design in a typeface of your choice.

way to organize a gardening scrapbook. Also try alternative groupings such as: perennials, bulbs, shrubs or flowers, fruits, vegetables.

If you have a pile of magazine clippings along with photographs, seed packages, and journal entries to place in your scrapbook, a three-ring binder is accommodating. It is capable of holding pocket folders, single pages, and folded pages. Photos can be mounted on single pages while pocket folders hold clippings and other loose items. A large garden schematic can be punched with three holes, folded in half and attached to the binder. If you have extra-large photographs and drawings that you want to lie flat, oversized scrapbooks are available.

Pressed flower with insect and heart confetti.

When designing the cover or title page, coordinate the imagery and idea with the theme of your scrapbook. A photograph of your garden or individual blossoms are natural images for the cover.

For lettering titles, calligraphy has an appropriate organic visual quality. Trust your own handwriting as well—it's bound to look "natural." Try a variety of pens, markers, and crayons and write out several examples in an extra-large size. Pick out the best and reduce on a copy machine. The reduction will tighten the lettering and give it a crisp look.

Alternatively, you can cover an album with handmade or mechanically made papers printed with patterns or flowers. Botanical wallpaper is durable yet appealing. You can buy a large sample piece to use as a cover for about one dollar. A single botanical drawing also makes an exquisite cover. The classic watercolor paintings of Graham Stewart Thomas, for example, can be photocopied, adhered to heavy weight paper, and glued to the cover.

GENEALOGICAL/FAMILY ARCHIVES SCRAPBOOK

Our Family History

Visit a local arboretum and take your own photograph of a majestic oak for a symbolic genealogical scrapbook cover or title image.

Some families can trace their history back for centuries. Others may only have records going back several generations. In either case, with some intrepid research, gathering, and editing, a genealogical scrapbook is slated for heirloom status.

Pages for the family archives can include:

- *The family crest.*

- *Visual or diagram of the genealogical line.*

- *An account of the family history.*

- *A list of family professions, achievements, and awards.*

- *Birth dates categorized by the month or season—perhaps everyone was born in the spring!*

- *Handwritten or printed letters, postcards, telegrams, invitations, greeting cards, and recipes that document historic moments in the family or create a written record.*

- *Photocopies of official documents concerning births, religious confirmations, marriages, home ownership, school and college records, military service, political offices, taxes.*

- *Newspaper articles about family members or activities.*

- *Photographs, drawings, prints of family members.*

- *Photographs of homes and antique items.*

- *Maps circling the locations of generations of family members.*

Photocopy important family records and overlap with relevant photographs.

Chronological order is the most logical choice for a genealogical scrapbook but it is not the only configuration. You could start with photographs and a diagram of the family tree, then on subsequent pages combine generations according to gender, profession, or special circumstances (all those who served in wars, all the artists, the sportsmen, for instance) rather than their year of birth. Another method is to give each individual their own page(s) or group nuclear families together. A good conclusion is the latest group photograph taken at a family reunion.

When the United States became involved in the European chapter of World War II, alien residents in the US who were from non-allied countries, were required to register with the Federal Government. Although grandfather Francesco had applied for and was granted citizenship, grandmother Rosa had not applied. She had been in the US for three years when she was called to complete alien registration. She was very frightened with thoughts of deportation back to war ravaged Italy. Of course, grandmother complied but then lived many years with her fear. The government kept the practice for quite some time after the war and so she carried the card with her always.

Application filed with the Alien Registration Division; Copy filed with the FBI office in Newark, NJ.

The family history in story and pictures. Original documents might be too fragile for a scrapbook but photocopy enlargements take their place in an album. Unlike an original document, photocopies can be edited, cut into parts, and mounted in a collage.

Because many old photos and antique items are included in a genealogical scrapbook, you should take special care to make sure that binding materials are of the highest archival quality. Select both papers and adhesives that won't destroy the scrapbook pages or the valuable memorabilia.

A definite cover image for your genealogical scrapbook is the family crest. Other images such as an engraving of a beautiful ancient oak tree can represent the extended family in a symbolic way. A map of the country of origin with the home city/town circled in red is another idea. Or simply write or stamp the family name in gold ink or marker.

Ancestral House c.1659

Photo silhouette of the family homestead.

GOLF SCRAPBOOK

A photo close-up and large graphic type make a bold cover.

Most golfers claim that their chosen sport is not just a game, it's a lifestyle. Saving score cards, keeping tabs on personal progress and achievements, and collecting memorabilia from various golf courses comes naturally to any player. A golfing scrapbook is about a round of days spent in the company of friends and colleagues while playing a most intriguing game.

Par for your scrapbook pages:

* *Scorecards from favorite games.*

- Ball markers.

- Receipts from golf club purchases.

- Packaging from golf balls and/or other items can be cut up and used to add color to pages. We're pretty sure it's impossible to put an actual golf ball in your scrapbook but a photo is a good substitute.

- List of favorite courses, locations, dates played, and any notes on the game.

- Photographs of courses with anecdotal information. Disposable panoramic cameras are terrific if you want a wide-angle view. Corresponding size photo sleeves are available for mounting them in your scrapbook. You can also take a series of overlapping shots and cut and paste them together for a handmade panorama.

- Photographs of the golfers at play or in the clubhouse. Try a few close-up shots of the player gripping the club or in swinging action to add variety.

- For those who have trouble keeping the ball on the fairway, a list of your worst "lies" and other great personal golfing achievements.

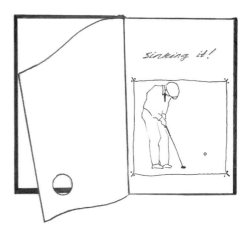

A hole-in-one scrapbook idea. A circle cut out of the page on the left will cover everything but the ball in the photo at right—until you turn the page to reveal the whole story.

- Brochures from favorite golf clubs.

- Drawings or diagrams of various golf courses of particular interest.

- Autographs and photos of professional players.

- Quotes and quips from favorite players.

- When a golf book makes the bestseller list (which seems to happen more and more frequently!), remember to copy the list for your scrapbook.

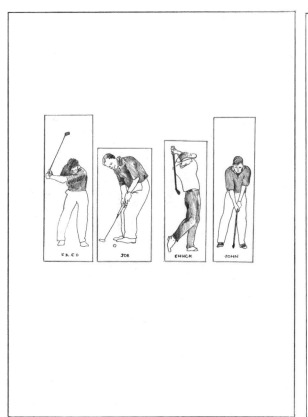

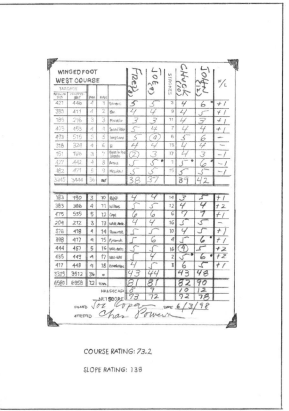

To keep both sides of a score card accessible, mount with photo tabs for easy removal. Write helpful or significant information around the card and add a photocopy of the golf club logo. At left, cut your photographs in long vertical strips to emphasize golfing positions.

- *Ticket stubs and souvenirs saved from professional tournaments.*

- *Antique golfing memorabilia purchased at auction or otherwise—if you can find a Bobby Jones scorecard, it's a scrapbook hole-in-one.*

- *Newspaper and magazine clippings on the game or favorite players.*

- *Great golfing statistics.*

A perfect scrapbook for a golfing fanatic consists of alternating sky blue and grass green pages. Available through art supply stores, Canson cotton papers have exceptionally good color quality and variety. For a custom bound album, check your local phone book or art center for crafts people who have skill in hand bookbinding. But if you feel adventurous, try making a book yourself. Many hand sewn or adhesive bindings are quite easy. Pauline Johnson's *Creative Bookbinding* is a good basic guide.

A store-bought album works nicely too. You can slip sheets of green paper into mylar pockets or paint a few white pages with green watercolor. But note: the latter will cause some wrinkling of the paper.

Inside your scrapbook, an interesting spread of two facing pages could consist of photographs mounted on blue color paper on the left and printed materials placed on green sheets to the right. Cut photos into long vertical strips to emphasize the individual golfers or various stances struck by an individual. Add handwritten captions to annotate the images and materials: "Don't be fooled by his great follow-through posture, Lloyd 'whiffed' that ball!" Date your materials as well: don't you want to keep track of how long it takes your game to improve?

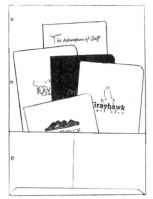

To keep your bulkier memorabilia visible and easy to reach, place in a large envelope cut open on one side.

HOLIDAY SCRAPBOOK

A hard-bound scrapbook personalized with a photograph from home.

An elaborate barbecue on the Fourth of July, a gracious formal dinner at Thanksgiving, and the many meals and parties shared during holidays are always cause to bring out a camera, make decorations, send invitations, uncork bubbly drinks, and have a wonderful time in the company of family and friends.

Take extra delight in the festivities many times over by creating a holiday scrapbook for all these marvelous events. So important are holidays, each one deserves its own album!

Decorate your holiday scrapbook pages with:

- *Photographs, photographs, and more photographs. Along with the traditional group shots and predictable poses, take some pictures at unusual angles: shoot from a second floor window and have everyone look up. Hold the camera above your head and point the lens into the party . . . yes, some pictures will not be usable but others will be surprisingly attractive and unique. Wide angle compositions are fun too— there are disposable cameras with this capability if you don't own a wide-angle lens.*

- *Photographs of decorations from around your house and neighborhood.*

- *Greeting card collages. Include those received and those you sent.*

- *Invitations to special dinner parties, guest lists, accompanying photos, menus, and wine labels.*

- *Photographs of table settings.*

- *Songs, prayers, and poems that have particular significance.*

- *Historic notes on the holiday.*

Flags flying on the Fourth

Neighborhood decorations on the Fourth of July. Photos have been cut out of their usual rectangular frame.

- *Contemporary and antique postage stamps and postcards commemorating the holiday.*

- *List of gifts sent and received.*

This playful montage of images celebrates a family holiday party. Photographs of people and food—in different sizes and scale—are cut into silhouettes and arranged on a page. Stars for the Fourth of July decorate the background. At right, make your own holiday scrapbook page markers using stickers and cardstock paper.

- *Gift tags and interesting package wrappings.*

- *Pressed flowers from centerpieces.*

- *Decorative embellishment can be added with holiday stickers, cookie cutters as a drawing template, metallic color pens, novelty edge rulers and scissors, craft punches, rubber stamps, stencils, and clip art; also consider cutting out shapes from wrapping papers, cards, and gift tags.*

A hard-bound, blank book lends itself nicely to the eclectic array of holiday scrapbook memorabilia. But many blank books have stock illustrations on the cover. If you find an album you like but the cover image is inappropriate for your needs, crop and glue your own photograph, drawing, or postcard over it. Wrapping paper or paper that you hand-painted, decoupaged, collaged, or decorated can replace the existing inside front and back covers. When complete, you'll have a professional looking custom book with little trouble.

If you choose to scrapbook many holidays together in one album, consider using a bookmark for an easy way of locating a specific seasonal event. A sticker or drawing placed at the top of a 4" x 2" long vertical strip of cardstock paper makes a good stiff insert to mark your scrapbook pages. Tucked into the gutter of the scrapbook or taped onto the page, it should protrude from the top of the scrapbook—just like the one you would use to mark your place after reading a novel. An alternative would be different color ribbons coordinated to the holiday. The ribbons can be glued to the page and hang loosely out of the bottom of the book to mark starting points.

LOVE SCRAPBOOK

Commercial papers printed with a variety of decorative images can be purchased at craft shops or art supply stores and make a good cover for a scrapbook of love.

Love appears in many forms: romance, familial love, and cherished friendships. Handmade scrapbooks are beautiful gifts to present to a loved one. Or make one for yourself to record a very special relationship. A romance scrapbook helps to chart the growth of love and becomes a keepsake for all the tender exchanges between a couple. A mother-daughter scrapbook makes a grand present for Mother's Day; the same holds true for sons, fathers, grandparents, aunts, uncles, and siblings or cousins.

Content for the pages of a romance scrapbook:

- *All the cards you exchange on Valentine's Day.*

- *Excerpts from love letters, notes, cards—or the complete letter if it's not too risqué!*

- *Enlarged copies of handwriting to highlight a significant compliment or proposal.*

- *A list of all the endearing salutations and closings from love letters: "Dearest," "My Sweet Kitten," "Hello Darlin'," "Love you from here to Pluto," "Every minute yours."*

- *Photographs of the couple in all their favorite places.*

- *A photomontage of shared activities such as ski trips, snorkeling, hiking, museum visits or dancing. It's fun to have a progression of photos taken over time such as a series showing the first session of learning the Fox Trot to pictures of the dancing couple winning an amateur competition.*

- *Little drawings, doodles, and stickers.*

- *Ticket stubs from concerts, lectures, and sporting events.*

ASHLEY DISCOVERS HER NEW BROTHER, BRANDON

Cute, cute little brother. How did you get here? You'll be my little plaything. And I won't keep you up at night. Cute, cute little brother. Where did you come from? Hey little brother, you're the sweetest thing I know. See him smile. See him gurgle. Cute, cute little thing. And I won't keep you up at night. Mommy and Daddy like to watch you all day. So cute little brother. Why do they watch you all day? See him smile. Hey little brother you're the sweetest thing I know.

Type a little story about a special moment and mount it with a photograph to document sibling love. Add stickers or mylar confetti and trim with decorative scissors for a tender touch.

- *Matchbooks, napkins, and business cards from favorite restaurants.*

- *Hotel stationery, brochures, photos, and other printed materials from romantic vacations.*

- *Descriptions of menus describing your most romantic dinners.*

- *Labels from wine or champagne bottles.*

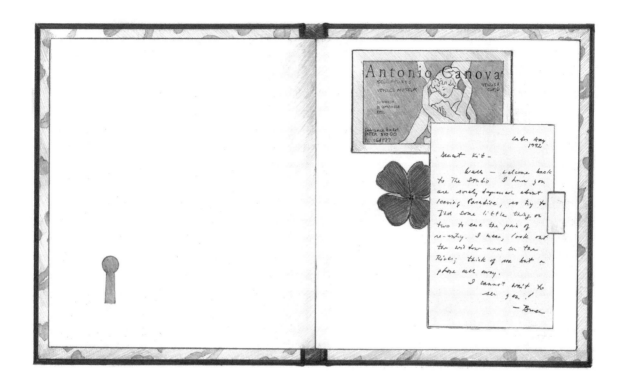

A special romance can be recorded in a scrapbook to keep the sentiments vivid. The ticket stub from an art exhibit, a love letter, and a pressed flower are arranged into a neat collage. The ticket and flower are glued to the page but the letter is taped so it can be lifted to show the complete image below. On the left facing previous page is a "keyhole" cut out. It reveals a secret peek of the collage page.

- *Pressed flowers from bouquets and the accompanying cards.*

- *A list of gifts exchanged and the ribbons and clippings from the wrapping.*

- *Meaningful song lyrics, poems, and special quotes.*

- *Reproductions of famous paintings or sculptures depicting great lovers. Rodin's "The Kiss" is perhaps the quintessential passionate embrace created by an artist. Antonio Canova's "Venus and Cupid" is quite loving and delicate as well.*

Print out bold letters on color paper and rearrange into an out-of-the-ordinary vertical composition. Add your own drawings of hearts.

Photos from romantic weekends and menus from favorite restaurants can be grouped in separate sections of the scrapbook. Cards and other letters can be photocopied, edited, compiled, and placed in a collage on a single page or a spread of facing pages. Or items might appear one to a page for dramatic focus.

A love song can conjure many heartfelt memories. Use a page of sheet music or a handwritten copy of lyrics to make an emotionally thoughtful cover or title page for your romance scrapbook. Another cover option is an enlargement of a love letter or a collage of many letters. One photograph of the couple engaged in a loving kiss can speak volumes.

This is a scrapbook whose theme begs to be contained in a beautiful one-of-a-kind hand-bound book. You can treat yourselves and order a special custom-made album from one of the companies on page 246.

NEW HOUSE SCRAPBOOK

What better way to title your new house scrapbook than with a welcoming portal?

Buying a house is a huge step for most. All the time you carefully spent looking for a residence can be captured on paper and bound for all to see and share. How else will you remember that the day you moved, it was pouring rain, and the moving truck got stuck in the mud of the dirt driveway—halfway uphill to the house.

Pages under your scrapbook roof can contain:

- *Before and after shots. Before: photographs of various views of the new house from the outside and the interior, before you move in. Don't forget the one with the "For Sale/Sold" sign. After: your*

new house once you've made it "yours" by dec-
orating, painting, and living in it a bit.

- *The computer print-out or newspaper advertis-*
  ing the house and listing its vital statistics.

- *A list of the houses you also considered or put*
  offers on.

- *A journal of house search stories; your notes on*
  each candidate.

- *A copy of the purchase agreement, certificate of*
  occupancy, and other related printed materials.

- *A photograph of closing day at the lawyer's*
  office (if you can stand it!).

- *A photograph of the previous owners and their*
  forwarding address (just in case you can't find
  the sump pump or find an item they left behind).

- *Photographs of the "fun" of moving day, includ-*
  ing at your former residence. Remember those
  friends who were teary-eyed to see you go?

- *Your change of address announcement.*

- *Letters, notes, and cards of congratulations*
  from family and friends.

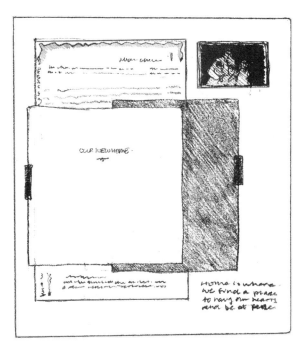

On a single page, copies or originals of significant paperwork
are combined with photos and handwritten notes. The papers
are attached on one side with archival tape and lay over one
another. They can be lifted to read the information below.

- *Swatches and samples of fabric, paint, carpet,*
  etc., for decorating schemes and color combina-
  tions; floor plans with possible furniture
  arrangements.

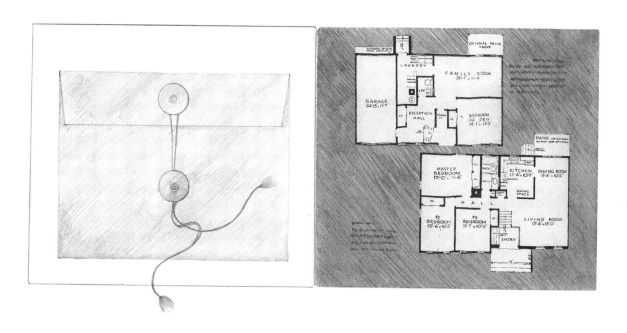

At right, house plans are copied and reduced to fit in your scrapbook, while the originals or other important papers remain in an envelope on a facing page. Envelopes of a variety of colors, sizes, and shapes are available through better stationery and office stores. Gold tassels on this envelope give it an official look.

A new house scrapbook is likely to include a good number of photographs. Pages created for three-ring binders have formats of one to six pockets which easily organize several different styles of photos including long horizontals and standard 4" by 6" rectangles. The multiple pockets lend themselves to tidy organization of images. Combine photo pockets with single pocket pages. The latter can be fitted with archival paper for mounting printed items such as the mortgage papers.

A photograph of the front door of your new home is the perfect cover image. If you stand on a small stool (if you are 6' 7" tall, the stool is not necessary) and point your camera slightly downward, your angle will impart a sense of entering the house. Unless you are a professional photographer, the chance of capturing a perfect composition in one try is unlikely. Shoot a whole roll of film with different exposures, at various times of day, preferably during bright but cloudy weather. Choose the best photo for your cover or title page. If you happily discover that you have ten good ones, glue them onto postcards and send them off to friends with your change of address. Be sure to save a postcard for your scrapbook as well.

A drawing of your new cottage is a personal record far more intimate than a photograph. If you can't draw yourself, commission a small illustration from a local artist.

OFFICE SCRAPBOOK

A handsome leather-bound book makes a great office scrapbook. Hot glue the company logo to the cover for a customized effect.

It might be that you work in a small business, large company, or a giant corporation. Whichever the case, a friendly bond naturally develops between colleagues joining together to achieve common goals. A scrapbook project recognizes accomplishments and celebrates the hard work of the team.

The pages of the office scrapbook could include:

- *A copy of company stationery and employee business cards.*

- *Publicity materials.*

- *An office timeline or brief history.*

- *Copies of the office newsletter or monthly report.*

- *Group and individual photographs, and those of special events such as conventions, conferences, the time a gorilla was hired to sing happy birthday to the office manager, or the hilarious inter-office softball league playoffs.*

- *Significant paperwork (plenty of that in any office) on a particular high point, e.g. a letter or contract accepting a bid on a new project.*

- *Certificates of achievement, letters of congratulations, or photocopies of award plaques.*

- *Important inter-office memos. And goofy memos and jokes sent around to maintain morale and keep things moving under stress.*

- *A humorous, out of context montage of employees: copy photos of individuals, cut out their faces, and glue them onto clip art or a reproduction of a famous painting. "George Washington Crossing the Delaware" is a heroic choice.*

An office journal of monthly activity combined with related photos.

- *Personal quotes and quips about office life . . . "If I'd known all this beforehand I wouldn't have taken the job!"*

- *Newspaper and magazine clippings reporting on or reviewing the company.*

Upper left layout

ANNUAL OFFICE PICNIC

Thrills	Spills	Good times
This year's annual picinic was held in a very special place. We went white water rafting in the "wild country" of the Rogue River refuge. What a blast! No one was allowed to talk about work. But we all did anyway	along with lots of screaming — as we worked our way down the river rapids. Rose kept getting into a jam here or there because she insisted on her own kayak. While the rest of us were in two group rafts. Ryo lead the	way in his tricornerd hat. Mike kept us from doing anything too stupid. Jessie fell out once and clung to a rock, refusing to swim until Mary came to her rescue. Paddling was a lot of work but the men split up so no

Upper right layout

ANNUAL OFFICE PICNIC

Thrills	Everything Else
This year's annual picinic was held in a very special place. We went white water rafting in the "wild country" of the Rogue River refuge. What a blast! No one was allowed to talk about work.	But we all did anyway along with lots of screaming — as we worked our way down the river rapids. Rose kept getting into a jam here or there because she insisted on her own kayak. While the rest of us were in two group rafts. Ryo lead the way in his tricornerd hat. Mike kept us from doing anything too stupid. Jessie fell out once and clung to a rock, refusing to swim until Mary came to her

Lower left layout

ANNUAL OFFICE PICNIC

This year's annual picinic was held in a very special place. We went white water rafting in the "wild country" of the Rogue River refuge. What a blast! No one was allowed to talk about work. But we all did anyway along with lots of screaming — as we worked our way down the river rapids. Rose kept getting into a jam here or there because she insisted on her own kayak. While the rest of us were in two group rafts. Ryo lead the way in his tri-cornerd hat. Mike kept us from doing anything too stupid. Jessie fell out once and clung to a rock, refusing to swim until Mary came to her rescue. Paddling was a lot of work but the men split up so no one would be lagging behind. The weather was so beautiful we all felt refreshed, rejuvenated, inspired and ready to tackle all our new projects. Let's do it again!

Lower right layout

Thrills	Spills	Good times
This year's annual picinic was held in a very special place. We went white water rafting in the "wild country" of the Rogue River refuge. What a blast! No one was allowed to talk about	work. But we all did any-way along with lots of screaming — as we worked our way down the river rapids. Rose kept get-ting into a jam here or there because she insisted on her own kayak. While	the rest of us were in two group rafts. Ryo lead the way in his tricornerd hat. Mike kept us from doing anything too stupid. Jessie fell out once and clung to a rock, refusing to swim until Mary came to her

ANNUAL OFFICE PICNIC

There is more than one way to set columns of type. Clockwise from upper left: three columns with vertical lines to separate text with photos cut to correspond; two columns of unequal size to place emphasis on one particular event over another; one large column of type in harmonious contrast with a group of little photos; three columns with the title at the bottom and a single photo silhouette.

A leather-bound album with leather tie closures makes a handsome presentation for an office scrapbook. For an aesthetically pleasing title, gold or opaque lettering or graphics (the company logo) can be stamped on the surface by the manufacturer. If you are concerned about wear and tear or cost, less-expensive binders come in synthetic materials that have the look and feel of real leather but wipe clean of fingerprints. To place a title on a synthetic surface, first glue the company logo or printed name onto a two-ply mat board. Cut to size. Use hot glue to adhere the board onto the cover.

A timeline of office activities and events is the most logical way of arranging an office scrapbook. After collecting your memorabilia, divide the materials into various categories. Sort each pile into chronological order. Once you do this, an arrangement is easy to coordinate and to maintain even when employees leave and are replaced by newcomers.

ALAN NEVER FALLS APART AT DEADLINE...

Cut up and caption your photos to illustrate a funny office moment.

PET SCRAPBOOK

Fun with word play: replace a title letter with a photograph of your pet.

Pedigreed or from the pound, our beloved pets have amazingly distinct personalities. Why not give them a scrapbook of their very own? All the joys of watching them play, cuddle, and explore can be annotated and stored in an album. Keep your scrapbooks in plain view for family members or any visitor to pick up and enjoy.

On the pages of a pet scrapbook you can place:

- *Photographs of your pet engaged in all the activities: at play, eating, sleeping, and interacting with people. If available, a group of photos* from infancy to the present reminds us of how quickly they grow.

- Drawings created by family members.

- Papers signifying pedigree.

- Information on lineage. Pet family tree.

- Information about the breed.

- Story of the adoption into the family.

- A lock of fur.

- Veterinary records and stories.

- Stories about curious habits and personalities.

- A list and packaging of favorite toys and foods.

- Photos of your pet on vacation.

- Old tags or collars.

A spiral-bound, blank book lends itself nicely to an eclectic array of scrapbook materials. Look for a book with a smooth, plain paper cover so you can add your personal style.

Give your pet a "voice" with the help of graphic balloons like those found in comic strips.

For a playful title, cut the letters of the name of your pet out of photographs. Bold sans serif typefaces such as Futura or Helvetica work best. First, print out the letters. Next, use a pencil and translucent vellum to trace an outline of a letter. Place the traced letter over a photo. Move the vellum across the image searching for areas that fit the letter forms and incorporate as much of the recognizable features as possible. When you find a suitable spot on the photograph, hold

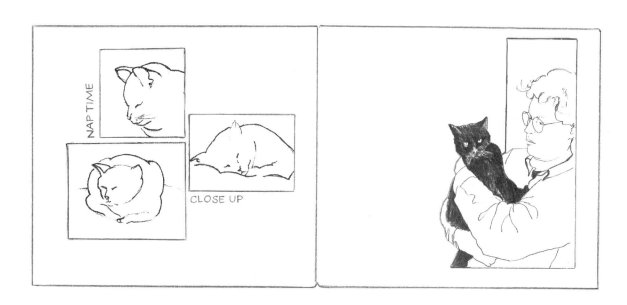

On the left, close-up photographs of your pet showing the various aspects of a particular behavior. On the right, cut photographs to silhouette and emphasize the animal.

or tape the vellum in place and draw over the outline with a ballpoint pen. The pressure from the pen will leave an incised line on the photo. Careful! Once you press with a hard tip pen, your photograph cannot be recovered. Follow the incised line and cut out the photo-lettering. Assemble the letters into the name and glue onto the title page of your scrapbook. A variation: choose one letter to cut from a photo and make the rest out of colorful paper.

Arrange the contents of your scrapbook to tell the story of your pet in pictures, drawings, and words. Begin with a description of adoption or birth followed by photos and drawings that illustrate the various aspects of your pet's personality and life in your home.

To enliven pages, break away from standard photo rectangles by cutting them into silhouettes or shapes such as diamonds, circles, ovals, stars, hearts, etc. For fun,

annotate the images in the voice of your pet: "Meeeeow, I'm Pumpkin. Can you believe the silly name I have just because my fur is orange!" Or, give your pet the ability to "speak" by adding balloon graphics like those found in comic strips: "Would someone please tell my master I do not like running into the water to catch my ball?"

Decorative paper frames a poignant moment.

POLITICAL SCRAPBOOK

For a patriotic cover or title page, cut letters from stars and stripes wrapping paper. Remove pins from the back of campaign buttons in order to glue flat.

"A vote for the Independent Ticket insures that all people will be represented."

Whether local or national, the business of government affects our lives every day. Rooting for a politician (or running for office yourself) and charting an election or term of office can become a patriotic scrapbook and can be kept as a personal and historical record.

Your scrapbook campaign pages could include:

* Bumper stickers, buttons, balloons, key chains, and T-shirts. Photocopies of anything too bulky for the album.

- *Newspaper clippings.*

- *Formal and informal photographs of the candidate or elected official.*

- *Preview ballot or actual paper ballot.*

- *Campaign literature.*

- *Photographs of election day, celebrations, yourself at voting booth.*

- *Letters from and to the politicians.*

- *Transcripts of speeches.*

- *Invitations to fund-raisers and inaugural ceremonies.*

- *Awards, ribbons.*

- *Posters and other memorabilia of the political party of your choice.*

- *Voting record of the candidate.*

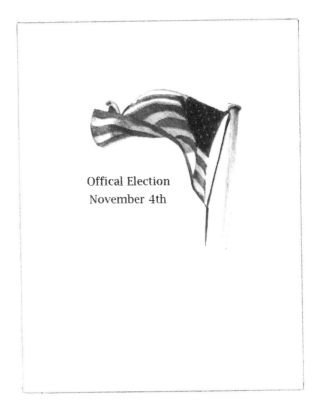

Offical Election
November 4th

Flag photo silhouette with printed type makes a good opener for your politics-as-usual scrapbook.

An oversized album makes a big statement for your political scrapbook. The long vertical pages can comfortably hold full-size newspaper pages and legal size papers. A 25" by 20" book is available through Light Impressions in Rochester, NY (the only source we know of that carries one this big). See page 247.

At left, the campaign newsletter was glued along the vertical edge and folded under itself. It can be unfolded to read the remaining portion. At right, dark color pages in your scrapbook add dramatic contrast when paired with light color items such as this black and white photograph and pink ribbon. The space between the text of the newsletter and the photo creates essential "breathing room" in the page design.

Alternatively, office supply stores carry large ring binders in many colors. For a patriotic grouping, divide your materials into three binders that have red, white, and blue covers. Each binder can focus on a particular aspect of your collection. The red binder can hold newspaper articles and ads. Bumper stickers, buttons, and other campaign ephemera for the blue binder. And the white binder can contain speeches and voting information. If you are storing the scrapbook on a shelf, print out lettering for the spine of the album for easy identification. To rotate type to fit vertically, you'll need a specialized computer application for achieving special effects with type. But you can choose small lettering and mount the type horizontally, if type-manipulation software is not available.

It seems fitting to adopt the flag for the title image of your scrapbook. Wait for a mildly windy day and take a photograph of "Old Glory" waving. Center the image on the page within a dignified frame. Or, for a more dramatic effect, enlarge the photograph and have it fill the page. Print the name of the politician black on white paper, cut into a horizontal strip and place over the flag at the bottom right. The name can easily be read but should not disrupt the image.

Another possibility is an enlargement of the Democratic or Republican icons, a donkey or an elephant. But only if you're a diehard member of either party. You wouldn't want to be stuck with a "white elephant" scrapbook!

READING SCRAPBOOK

Cut letters from decorative paper or a page of text, then glue to the cover of your scrapbook for a readable title.

Did you ever want to recall all the wonderful books you've read over the years only to find that your mind draws a blank? Or do you have the titles of memorable books scribbled on stray pieces of paper and stashed out of sight at the bottom of a box of miscellaneous items?

A reading scrapbook is a useful, pleasing, and visible way to keep track of all the meaningful books, essays, and articles that you want to remember and share.

If you never jotted down the names of authors

or titles of works that you've read and can't seem to remember them all, try gathering your friends together for a "recall session." Sitting in the living room with a cup of coffee and exchanging reading reminiscences will help shake up settled memories and start a good list of books for your scrapbook. And don't forget to simply turn to your own collection, perhaps everything you need is resting on the bookshelves.

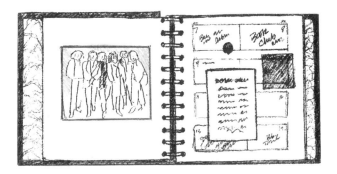

Recycle a weekly date book into your reading scrapbook. Glue notes and other mementos directly over calendar entries leaving relevant dates visible. Adhere your own photographs over the existing printed images if you prefer.

Pages of your scrapbook could list and picture:

- *Color photocopies of book jackets reduced in size to allow for several images on a page.*

- *A single book jacket with accompanying anecdotal information such as the year you read it, where you were, how you felt.*

- *Photographs of authors copied from the back of book jackets.*

- *Photographs or portrait drawings of authors clipped from newspapers or magazines.*

- *Newspaper or magazine reviews.*

- *The most meaningful quotes and passages from each book.*

- *A list of authors with their work divided into categories such as novels, short fiction, poetry, or essays.*

- *Lists of books categorized by genre such as mystery or romance.*

- *Books and authors recommended by friends.*

- *Articles pulled from magazines and saved in their entirety.*

BOOK CLUB SELECTIONS 1995-1996

MONKEYS
STILL LIFE
POSSESSION
SPORTSMAN'S PARADISE

FAMILY HAPPINESS
REFUGE
ELLEN FOSTER
THE PRIMARY COLORS

That's us between titles.

What better place to play with typography than in a reading scrapbook? At left, giant–size type in a bold sans serif face for a title page. The type was printed horizontally but mounted in a vertical direction. On the right, type in combination with handwriting and a cut photograph.

- *Ticket stubs from public readings you attended.*

- *Autographs of authors.*

- *Handwritten letters received from authors in response to your praise.*

- *Photocopy of a title page inscribed by the author. After waiting hours to have Frank McCourt sign your copy of* Angela's Ashes, *don't you want to have that page with his signature in your scrapbook?*

If you're involved in a book club, perhaps you and the other members would like to start a group scrapbook to keep track of what you've read, discussion topics, and club refreshments.

An expandable or three-ring binder is best for a reading scrapbook. As your list of favorite books grows so can your scrapbook. Decide on the order and organization of your pages after surveying your contents. If you have a colossal list of books and materials you could have more than one scrapbook, each with a theme such as women authors or critical essays. If your materials and lists are small perhaps you can compose your scrapbook by year, e.g. all the great novels you read during the Winter of 1998. Since a reading scrapbook involves language, another option would be to organize the contents alphabetically, either by author or title.

The cover of a reading scrapbook can vary widely from a simple hand-lettered title, "READ," to an elaborate collage of authors' photographs, signatures, and quotes. A subtle play on words would be a scrapbook with a solid red cover, to signify the books you have "read."

Old books often have embossed or textured covers. Place paper over the book cover and rub into it using a soft crayon. An image will rise and make an artistic record of one of your favorite titles.

RESTAURANT SCRAPBOOK

JAVA JOINT

ANCHOR INN

Villa de Napoli

KENNY'S

Benj

Table For 2

roselli's

Collect stationery and logos for a restaurant scrapbook title. Cut up the objects, glue to a single piece of paper, and color copy to eliminate raw edges and leave the page looking smooth.

If eating out is one of your favorite hobbies, and you keep a basket full of notes on the fabulous meals and wines you've enjoyed, you are a candidate for keeping a special scrapbook. Gathering restaurant memorabilia not only gives you the opportunity to relive a great meal, your collective effort becomes a vivid, reliable resource for family and friends in search of good restaurants.

On the pages of your restaurant scrapbook you can place:

• *Original menus or reduced copies. Your local*

copy center can color copy and reduce an image—usually for less than a dollar.

- A list of the specialties you enjoyed during a specific meal, with your own notes and comments. Feel free to include your bad reviews. One scrapbooker mounted the business card of an Italian restaurant called "Titanic," with the caption: "The restaurant was like its name: it sunk!"

- Photographs taken at the restaurant (don't forget a shot of the exterior sign) and with the chef. A kitchen photo is difficult to obtain but you can always ask. Photograph the plate of food as well. It's nice to recall the chef's presentation.

- Drawings of food, if you don't want to bring a camera along to the meal. Color copies of a few decorative images of food enliven pages of text.

- The itemized bill. This is especially entertaining if the restaurant is in a foreign country with different currency.

- Illustrations and recipes from books created by the restaurant chef. Mollie Katzen's Still Life with Menu has her own drawings and wonderful recipes from Moosewood, a restaurant she

Drawings of the food presentation help recall the flavors of the dish.

founded in Ithaca, New York.

- Business cards from the restaurant establishment, the chef, and other personnel.

- Wine labels, notes, and stories from the sommelier.

- Reviews of, recipes from, or articles about restaurants clipped from magazines and newspapers.

- A map of the country (or even the world!) with all the places you've dined highlighted. Perhaps you can find tiny stickers of forks or chef's hats to mark the locations.

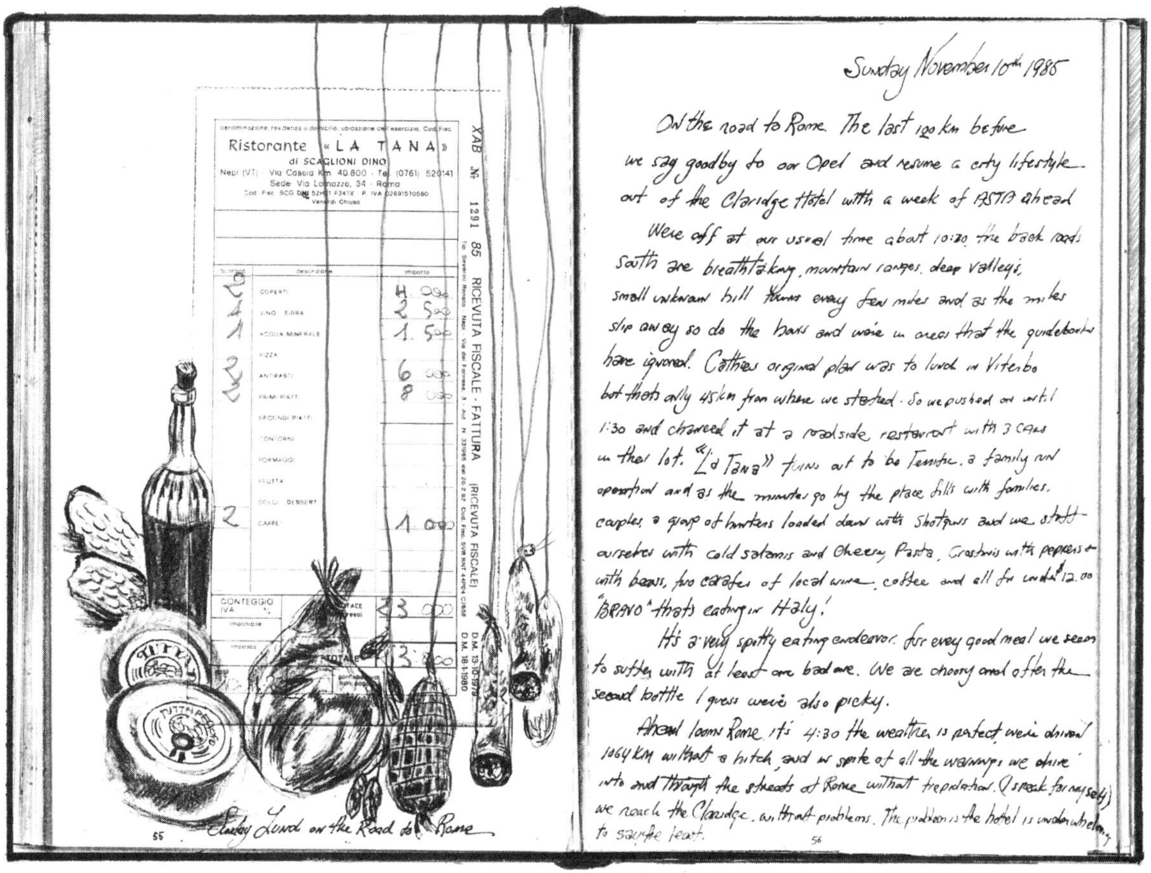

The left page shows a restaurant bill from "Ristorante «LA TANA»" and sketches of food items. The right page contains handwritten journal text.

Ristorante «LA TANA»
di SCAGLIONI DINO
Nepi (VT) - Via Cassia Km. 40.800 - Tel. (0761) 520141
Sede: Via Lamozze, 34 - Roma

RICEVUTA FISCALE · FATTURA

descrizione	importo
COPERTI	4.00
VINO - BIRRA	2.50
ACQUA MINERALE	1.50
PIZZA	
ANTIPASTO	6.00
PRIMI PIATTI	8.00
SECONDI PIATTI	
CONTORNI	
FORMAGGI	
FRUTTA	
DOLCI - DESSERT	
CAFFE	1.00

Sunday November 10th 1985

On the road to Rome. The last 100 km before we say goodby to our Opel and resume a city lifestyle out of the Claridge Hotel with a week of PASTA ahead

We're off at our usual time about 10:30 the back roads south are breathtaking, mountain ranges, deep valleys, small unknown hill towns every few miles and as the miles slip away so do the bars and we're in areas that the guidebooks have ignored. Cathies original plan was to lunch in Viterbo but thats only 45 km from where we started. So we pushed on until 1:30 and chanced it at a roadside restaurant with 3 cars in the lot. "La Tana" turns out to be Terrific. a family run operation and as the minutes go by the place fills with families, couples, a group of hunters loaded down with shotguns and we stuff ourselves with cold salamis and Cheesy Pasta. Crostinis with peppers or with beans, two carafes of local wine, coffee and all for under $12.00 "BRAVO" thats eating in Italy!

It's a very spotty eating endeavor. for every good meal we seem to suffer with at least one bad one. We are choosy and after the second bottle I guess we're also picky.

Ahead looms Rome it's 4:30 the weather is perfect we've driven 1064 km without a hitch and in spite of all the warnings we drive into and through the streets of Rome without trepidation. (I speak for myself) we reach the Claridge. without problems. The problem is the hotel is underwhelming to say the least.

Early Lunch on the Road to Rome

55   56

A restaurant journal. Handwritten descriptive information about the meal arranged with the printed bill and sketches of the specific foods.

One way to create order in your restaurant scrapbook is by dividing the pages into geographical regions. Or you could group pages by the type of cuisine, such as Italian, Ethiopian, French, etc.

Ring binders that allow you to mix a variety of page formats into one book are a good choice for this project. To hold menus and/or magazine clippings, a 10" x 13" envelope can be punched with three holes to fit the ring clasps of the binding.

Cropped to focus on a particular aspect of the composition, photos and illustrations can be neatly aligned on pages along with corresponding business cards and bills of fare. Anecdotes about the meal can be printed on paper, cut, and glued onto the page near the photograph. For a relaxed design, cut silhouettes of food, people, and the restaurant exterior and montage the images together overlapping and fitting them in a casual arrangement. Use colorful felt-tip pens to write notes about the meal in and around the edges of your photos.

The striking diversity of this scrapbook calls for a title page that pulls the contents together. Use printed lettering or a calligraphic brush pen to write: "Great Restaurants & Remarkable Meals." A decorative border or frame placed around the lettering gives the composition a complete and finished appearance. Books are available that contain stock illustrations of decorative borders and edging. Look in the graphic design shelves of your local library or bookstore. The illustrations can be copied by machine or used as a model for your own hand drawings. Other tools for creating borders include acrylic rulers and templates and pre-printed laser papers, available through catalogs.

Cut out a photograph or postcard and combine with the bill from a special meal.

RETIREMENT HONOR SCRAPBOOK

An elegant leather-bound scrapbook with professionally embossed lettering and graphics.

A gold watch is nice. But a scrapbook that has been thoughtfully created by colleagues, family, and friends celebrates a retiree with the deepest heartfelt honor. Be prepared for an outpouring of emotion when the album is presented.

Scrapbook pages could include:

- *Photographs of the retiree in the workplace and on the road—from throughout his/her career. A professional photograph arranged as part of the retirement gift is an extra added touch, but you'll have to be a bit sneaky not to reveal the true purpose.*

- Letters or telegrams sending good wishes from colleagues, family, and friends.

- Business cards and company stationery.

- A timeline describing accomplishments.

- An old résumé from the retiree's early career days, along with the current version.

- Copies of awards, certificates, and letters of commendation received over the years.

- Letters of promotion. If you can't gain access to the retiree's files without giving away the surprise, then check the corporation files.

- Newspaper or magazine clippings relating to the person's career. If your retiree was a department store buyer, you could include articles on the entire fashion industry, not only her store.

- Letters written by the retiree musing over office activities.

- A list of the retiree's favorite, or infamous, expressions: "We're on a critical path." Or "It's huge!"

- The last page could contain a blank golf score card and wishes to break 100, a lottery ticket, a gift certificate, or a group photograph of colleagues waving a farewell.

JOSEPH GONNELLA

A LIFE AT THE PRESS

A simple title page for a retirement scrapbook. A photograph of the retiree is cropped so the figure breaks out of the usual rectangular frame.

HONORS

At the time of her retirement Robin Landa has

achieved the highest honors awarded in her profession.

GOLD METAL

She not only was admired for her great service she was

creative in every endeavor. Her awards include the gold

metal of service. The certificate of achievement and the

creative excellence for arts and letters. Congratulations.

A page of text outlining a retiree's career achievements is designed formally to reflect high honors. To achieve this dignified design, the title is centered right on the page and surrounded by free space. It points into the right page where printed type has been neatly arranged with wide spacing between each line.

- *If you're not going for a dignified theme, you could include funny cartoons pertaining to the workplace. Try the* New Yorker *or "Dilbert."*

- *See the* office scrapbook *on page 163 for additional ideas.*

An antique-looking leather bound book sends an instant message of respect to the scrapbook recipient. Tapestry coverings also have a time-honored, noble visual appearance. An excellent selection of elegant scrapbooks are stocked by better paper stores and archival merchandise retailers.

Gold foil lettering in a script typeface (Shelley Allegro or Bellevue, for example) can be printed on the title page of the scrapbook. The graceful style naturally complements a leather cover. With a little practice, you can use color foil transfer sheets and laser printers. For a totally professional finish, hire a calligrapher to create a custom design for the title page.

Instead of dwelling on the passage of time, arrange the retirement scrapbook in divisions based on the various categories listed above: career biography followed by sections on awards, photographs of colleagues, photos of the retiree, and letters of good wishes, etc. Each section can be titled in a script typeface. Enlarging the first letter of the word results in a dramatic initial capital: Awards 1957–1998.

Keep the placement of items simple. Single out each piece of memorabilia and mount on right pages only. This gives the letter or award certificate more significance. If a single photograph looks lost by itself, group several related images together in the center of the page, leaving an eighth of an inch spacing between them.

SCHOOL YEARS
SCRAPBOOK

LIFE
IN
CLASS
1965 - 1977

Glue a photocopy of a traditional black and white tablet notebook to the cover of a plain book or the first page of your album.

Is there a big box of mementos from your children's years at school tucked away on the top shelf of your closet? Did you save the items for sentimental reasons hoping to someday organize the photographs and memorabilia? A school years scrapbook gives these items a place to be seen and enjoyed. It also makes a charming graduation or wedding gift for your daughter or son.

Depending on the amount of materials saved, a school years scrapbook can span grade school through college or be divided into separate books based on graduation dates.

You can include:

- Clippings from the school newspaper or perhaps the last issue of the paper before graduation.

- Photos taken during the school years arranged in related groups: sports, clubs, ceremonies, and favorite teachers and mentors.

- Photos color copied from the printed school yearbooks; these photos can be reduced or enlarged and highlighted in a different way than in the official yearbook.

- A photograph of both the interior of the school and the outside building and grounds, including the school's name.

- Copies of merit certificates and diplomas, or if using the originals be sure to have an archivally safe binder.

- Programs from school plays, honor society banquets, sports ceremonies, dances, competitions.

- A record of courses taken, honorable grades

Annotate your images using a pen especially made for writing on photos. Add stickers for fun.

received, and anecdotes about the process.

- Poems, creative writing samples, essays, exams, drawings, and other items personally created.

- Notes from and photos of favorite teachers or other school personnel.

- A list of great scientists, authors, artists, or other individuals who were inspirational to the student. When the former students look back at this list after 20 years, they will be amazed to remember whose work was influential during their formative period.

Contrasting color pages in an album helps to distinguish the mounted items. At left, photos can be cut into shapes to highlight specific areas of importance. Separate your student within a group photo by cutting into the rectangle to reveal a silhouette of the figure. On the facing page, a single photo is surrounded by a description and images of honors and awards. The school emblem patch is glued above the photograph.

Combine printed materials such as award certificates or a program from the student play with photographs and arrange in a single collage. Or separate the items and neatly place on facing pages. You could even mimic the layout of a school yearbook, with small photos of your subjects and friends, listing their favorite memories and expressions beneath. Appoint an extra special item its own page and write in anecdotal information on the achievement: "Science lab has never been easy for Mary. But after studying and working every night for a month straight, she achieved the best in class for her lab report."

Different albums can be used for a school years scrapbook. Try a simple three-ring binder, expandable binders, or a mylar sleeve binder with black paper pages. This latter type is perfect for holding papers; photographs can be glued to the black paper and report cards, science papers, and other materials can be held without glue in the pockets of mylar. Printed materials such as programs from awards ceremonies are usually not archivally sound. Acidic materials need to be neutralized with a spray chemical for this purpose or photocopied onto archival paper.

The cover or title pages of a school years scrapbook can reflect the character of the content. A scrapbook from grade school could be lighthearted while one for college would be more "academic."

A college scrapbook cover can show the school emblem or an enlargement of one photo such as the student collecting his or her diploma at graduation. A high school varsity letter makes a bold statement attached to the cover of the book using hot glue.

Or a copy of a grade "A" report—enlarged for dramatic effect—can be glued to the title page.

SPECIAL OUTINGS
SCRAPBOOK

Playing with scale: Superimpose a photo silhouette of the family onto the cover of a nature reserve brochure. Then photocopy the montage for a wonderful title page.

Trips to the zoo, the science or art museum, aquarium, seaport, or a special visit to a city or nature center are delightful moments to document. Scrapbooking the record of these cherished mini-events keeps the experience close and reminds us of how important it is to take time to enjoy life together.

The scrapbook can be a large ongoing project, compiling memories of a variety of outings, or choose a little scrapbook to highlight one extra-special and enjoyable experience.

A trip to the city scrapbook could contain:

- *A map of the city or portion of the map with a red line tracing those areas visited—didn't you walk the freedom trail while you were in Boston?*

- *Visitor center brochures.*

- *Printed information from the local historic sites.*

- *A list of favorite places within the city and notes about what you enjoyed.*

- *Plenty of photographs of the architecture, street signs, landmarks, and the corner coffee shop where you learned some interesting facts from the local residents (don't forget a matchbook). It's fun to pose with the proprietor or waiters in the local establishments—everyone usually wants to cram into the picture.*

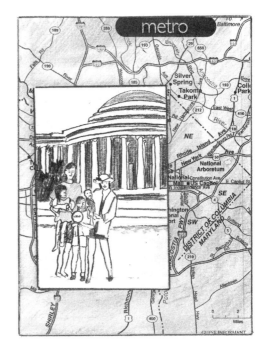

A map makes an eye-catching frame for a special family photograph.

Nature outings scrapbook pages hold:

- *Trail map and notes taken along the path.*

- *Brochures from the local conservation agency.*

- *Intimate close-up photographs of the flora of the area, as well as the spectacular distant views.*

- *Photographs of the walkers or hikers as they disappear down the trail into the woods.*

- *Notes on the natural history of the area.*

- *Sketches of leaves, flowers, nuts, or stones.*

- *While you want to respect the park ordinances and not remove any actual plants, you can make color copies from a field guide.*

QUAIL FEATHER

WATCH OUT FOR THAT TREE!

Contrasting color pages help to highlight specific items in your scrapbook. At top, a quail feather is fixed to the page with archival tape. Not all your scrapbook pages need to be filled up. At times, it's nice to leave lots of free space to spotlight one particular item.

A museum visit scrapbook has:

- *Postcard reproductions from the museum shop.*

- *Entrance ticket.*

- *A map of the museum with a few notes on each exhibit.*

- *Photographs outside the museum, in the cafeteria or cafe, and if permitted, in the exhibit.*

To compose your scrapbook pages, cut and combine printed materials such as a brochure or a map with photographs and place on a single page in a neat arrangement. Or separate the photographs from other materials and arrange on facing pages.

A three-ring binder is good for an outings scrapbook. It has pages for photographs and mylar envelopes can be added for bulkier materials. If your project is small in scope, you can choose a bound scrapbook which has a finite number of pages. Before gluing into this type of binder, planning is necessary to fill the book. If you have an abundance of materials, you'll need to edit or combine items. If you find that the book can't be filled, look over your materials, edit, and give them plenty of space, even one to a page. This will spread out the contents and fill the book. If you are concerned about a few blank pages left, simply but carefully cut them out of the book.

Choose a cover or title page appropriate for your subject. A decoupage of leaves or handmade papers with embedded petals and leaves make a beautiful cover for a nature scrapbook. Maps can be folded into a book covering for a city trip album. This type of cover is not glued; it is a slipjacket much like the book covers you once made to protect your grammar school texts.

SPORTS FAN SCRAPBOOK

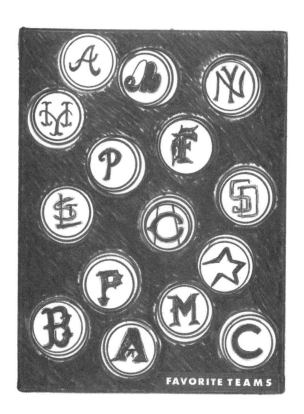

Cloth decals from professional teams are a champion sports fan's cover.

Are baseball cards, pennants, stat books, and autographed balls strewn about your bedroom? Is a hockey jersey your frequent attire? Then you or someone you know is a definite candidate for a sports fan scrapbook. The scrapbook might also evolve into a journal that keeps tabs on the fan's favorite activity from season to season.

Scrapbook pages can include:

- *Autographs of professional players.*

- *Programs from sporting events.*

- *A list of favorite players and their statistics.*

- *All kinds of photographs including the players, coaches, stadiums, and the sport fan at the events.*

- *Pennants and patches representing favorite teams.*

- *Ticket stubs from games with the final score for each team.*

- *Newspaper and magazine clippings about favorite players, coaches, teams.*

- *Treasured trading cards.*

A photograph of a professional athlete fills the page at left. At right, a collage of ticket stubs and programs.

The quantity and scope of the collected memorabilia will determine the arrangement. If the collection is vast, then separating the materials and photographs into a single sport or even a single team might be good.

A scrapbook can follow the careers of a few exceptional players such as a Wayne Gretzky scrapbook or a Michael Jordan scrapbook. Don't you wish your great-grandfather had made a Babe Ruth scrapbook?

A smaller collection might focus on either a chronology of sporting events by the season or by category such as statistics, autographs, ticket stubs, and photographs.

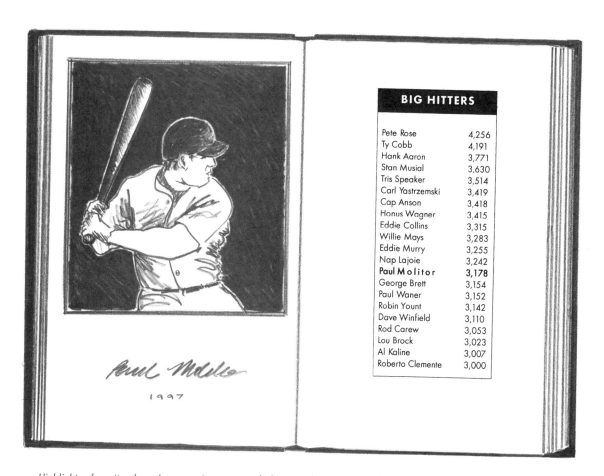

BIG HITTERS

Pete Rose	4,256
Ty Cobb	4,191
Hank Aaron	3,771
Stan Musial	3,630
Tris Speaker	3,514
Carl Yastrzemski	3,419
Cap Anson	3,418
Honus Wagner	3,415
Eddie Collins	3,315
Willie Mays	3,283
Eddie Murry	3,255
Nap Lajoie	3,242
Paul Molitor	**3,178**
George Brett	3,154
Paul Waner	3,152
Robin Yount	3,142
Dave Winfield	3,110
Rod Carew	3,053
Lou Brock	3,023
Al Kaline	3,007
Roberto Clemente	3,000

Highlight a favorite player by arranging an actual photograph or magazine image with an autograph and statistics. It's fun to see how the athlete rates in comparison to other players.

A collage of photographs, autographs, and ticket stubs can be temporarily composed, then photocopied for the cover image. The materials can then be dismantled from the collage and placed back inside the scrapbook on the appropriate pages. This sort of collage is also good for the inside covers of your scrapbook, when you use a single image for the cover.

Colorful team logos are a good choice for the scrapbook cover, too. The images can be collected and color photocopied to make them fairly equal in size. The logos can be casually arranged or in neat rows forming a grid. Some sports fans are fanatical about organization of their stats and memorabilia—others just like to stack it up. If you make the scrapbook as a gift, try to reflect the character of the recipient.

STYLE SCRAPBOOK

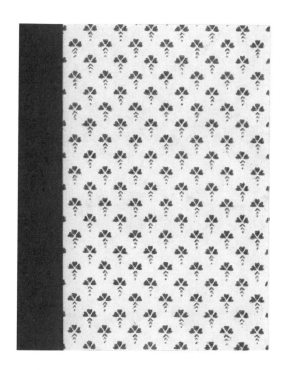

Wallpaper is an appropriate way to cover your style scrapbook. Adhere with archival glue or fold the paper and tuck into the front and back covers of the album.

We invest a great deal of time "feathering our nests" with care and love. Often, the process of searching for the perfect rug to match a long-sought sofa, picking comforting bed linens, and choosing an exquisite hand-painted tile for the kitchen is as much fun as finding those pieces. Scrapbooking the evolution of the right style for your home helps in the decorating process itself by serving as a permanent reference. Bring your style scrapbook along the next time you go shopping for your home. It will contain all the information you need to insure that you've indeed found the right color rug to match the new wall paint.

Good things for your scrapbook pages:

- *Paint chips from company brochures.*

- *Notes on color palettes. If you see a group of colors that interact well together, write down the name of each and then record with water-color or color pencil in your scrapbook.*

- *Fabric swatches.*

- *Magazine and catalog clippings of favorite inspiring home decorating ideas.*

- *A diagram of your floor plan with the relative fabric swatches on the facing page.*

- *Wallpaper samples.*

- *Manufacturers brochures of appliances or other home items. If you cut up the brochure, save the product numbers for later reference.*

- *Floor tile samples or color copies of the title.*

- *Photographs showing the before and after results of decorating.*

Record your decorating inspirations and ideas with pictures and color swatches. Above, handpainted cardboard chips to indicate the artist's color choices overlap a postcard reproduction of a famous French painting.

- *Close-up photos of single pieces. Use these for comparison while shopping for coordinating items.*

- *Sketches of custom-made items.*

- *Tips and techniques from experts.*

A LOVE STORY

WE HAD BEEN LOOKING FOR A KILIM RUG FOR OUR LIVING ROOM FOR A VERY LONG TIME. We looked at hundreds. And then, burnt out from the search, we decided we needed a rest. During that period we happened upon a film based on an Iranian fairy tale. The name of the film

was "Gabbeh." Within the plot of the story, a woman weaves a rug as part of her preparation for marriage. The rug must be made well to last a very long time. Anyway, the film was a love story and the rugs were just beautiful. "Gabbeh" then went into our heart and tucked away in our minds.

We started to search for our kilim a few weeks later and again were disappointed. On our way out to the door of what seemed like the hundredth shop, Bill spotted an interesting rug and said, "This one reminds me of "Gabbeh." Aaaahhh, said the rug salesman, you are right, but that is a copy. Come this way and I will show you something special. We followed him to the back of the shop where he uncovered (under stacks and stacks) a luxuri-

ous rug exactly like the one in "Gabbeh." We were awestruck. It was so sensuous in color and subtle in pattern. We had found our rug.

A style scrapbook journal. Combine stories of your significant decorating moments with a photographic enlargement. The photo fits snugly into the type with the help of page-layout computer software. Or print the type and cut it up to fit around the photograph.

- *Notes compiled from various books you consulted. Don't forget to jot down the title, author, and publisher. Several Scrapbook Guild members have found* Elegant and Easy Rooms *by Dylan Landis particularly useful.*

- *Quotes regarding the pleasures of domestic life. "Have nothing in your houses that you do not know to be useful, or believe to be beautiful." —William Morris.*

- *Stories of projects accomplished, including the frustrating moments. A reminder of how to avoid problems the next time.*

- *A list of future ideas and fantasies.*

Compile your scrapbook materials and sort by room, e.g. all the samples and inspirational photos for decorating the bath. It's best to keep related items in a single section to see how they interrelate.

For the album, your own hand-sewn book allows complete control of its style. Traditional Japanese binding techniques are uncomplicated and flexible. Thread and cover materials can be coordinated. Make the covers out of fabric, wallpaper swatches, or create your own decorated fabric or paper. Wax resists, stencil prints, sponging, decoupage, and marbleizing take time but are truly rewarding during the process and in the finished piece. You might even find a use for the prints in your home. See the chapter on decorative papers in Pauline Johnson's *Creative Bookbinding*. A tassel, fringe, or cording from a fancy upholstery shop makes a wonderful bookmark for your scrapbook. Attach the cord of the tassel to the inside spine and let it hang down through a set of pages. A stylish finish!

Keep your style scrapbook small in size. It will be easy to carry along on shopping forays.

Other style scrapbooks:
Fashion with clippings from
catalogs and magazines of your
favorite dresses and accessories,
your "colors," fabric swatches.
Table settings scrapbook with
notes on table etiquette, napkin
folding ideas, photos from
magazines, centerpiece ideas.

TEAM SPORTS
SCRAPBOOK

It's not just a game.

Baseball, soccer, basketball, and tennis ball photographs have been photocopied, cut into quarters, and remounted with colorful paper into a cohesive group.

Learning a sport, practicing with intense concentration, and finally making the team is a super achievement worth celebrating. Scrapbooking captures all the moments of team play and individual contributions and sets them in a permanent spot to admire. Your team sports scrapbook can highlight a single year or span the course of several. Save schedules, rule books, and team members' signatures to enrich the photographic entries of your album.

At play on the field of your scrapbook:

- *Formal and informal photographs of the team.*

- *Photos of team players in action.*

- *Team logos.*

- *Schedules from a season of games.*

- *Statistics.*

- *Notes on game rules with anecdotes about specific games where the rules were in question.*

- *Signatures of coaches and team members.*

- *Photos of uniforms.*

- *Programs from awards ceremonies.*

- *Photocopies of ribbons and other awards so they can be in your scrapbook as well as remain hanging on a bedroom wall.*

- *Information on the coaches and sponsors.*

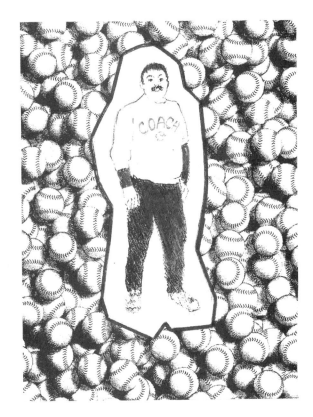

Honoring the team coach. Printed papers used as a background can decoratively frame simple photographs.

An album with saddle stitching is a sure hit for your team sports scrapbook. The tiny stitches around the border are reminiscent of those found on baseballs, soccer, and other sporting balls. You can hot glue an appliqué of the team logo to the cover. Or leave the cover as it is and place a bold title on the first page. A matte texture paper ring binder is

Instead of the usual stack of six rectangular photographs on a single page, make your scrapbook visually arresting by cutting your images into shapes and sizes.

another choice. It is easy to adhere photos and other printed materials to the cover with archival glue.

Instead of the usual arrangement of stacking of 4" x 6" photographs on a single page, cut out extraneous background to get the optimum visual impact from your images. You can also cut the photos into various shapes to complement the figure or object in the photograph. A team member in action could be cut into a parallelogram to echo the dynamic movement pictured. Or a photo of a T-shirt can be cut around the edges so it looks like the shirt itself. Have fun!

THEATER/CONCERT SCRAPBOOK

Let it all hang out. For the avid rock concert fan, a cover made from an actual pair of blue jeans, a bandanna, and a treasured ticket stub.

Collecting and saving playbills, ticket stubs, play lists, autographs, and photos of performers, and that receipt from a backstage pass does not necessarily indicate that the theater or music buff is a fanatic. But what about the time you were able to get Bruce Springsteen's bandanna or was it Pavarotti's handkerchief? When the quantity of material is bursting through the boxes in which they are stored and there are extra-special items that beg to be shared and displayed, it's time for a scrapbook.

On the center stage of your scrapbook pages you can include:

- *Playbills, programs, and librettos.*

- *Ticket stubs and a map of the theater's seating plan (or where you sat on the lawn for an outdoor concert).*

- *Reviews of the play or concert from newspapers and magazines.*

- *Pages from the script of a play.*

- *History notes. A trivia game would be fun to include in your scrapbook too. What actress inspired Puccini to compose an opera from the play in which he saw her perform? Or who was the opening act at Woodstock in '69?*

- *Copy of your own fan letters and any responses from the musician or actor.*

- *Autographed glossy photos and other gift shop items.*

- *Old high school or college yearbook photos of performers. (This is not as difficult as it may*

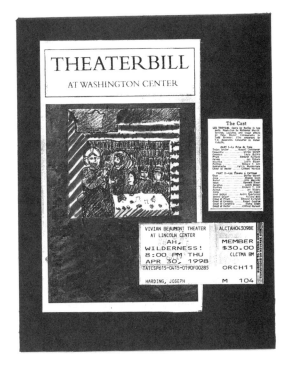

A theater program often has wonderful illustrations. Tear off the cover from the program—or color copy it—and arrange in a neat composition with your ticket stub and the cast list.

seem. Biographies of the performers usually include educational background. Call the school and ask if a copy is available in the library archive.)

A "mini-book" within your main scrapbook. For one performance you may have collected and saved a program, newspaper reviews, the ticket stub, and other items. To keep related pieces together, adhere a long accordion-folded paper to a single page of your scrapbook and mount a series of mementos one to a sheet.

- *Photographs you've taken of the theater, performers, or stage settings.*

- *Publicity materials from the orchestra, theater group, or performing arts center.*

- *A list of all the plays, concerts, or operas you attended in a given season.*

Gather your materials and organize your scrapbook by performance. Your photographs and printed items can be grouped on a single spread of pages or carried through to several. Pages could be arranged in even numbers to keep related items together. You can also organize your scrapbook around a single performer—all about Helen Hayes—or a particular playwright . . . How many times have you seen *Hamlet?*

Book post binders and ring binders are expandable and can accommodate heavier items such as playbills and librettos. But remember, these scrapbooks do have a maximum width. Limit your items by cropping photos to include the most significant information. Use a color or black and white copy machine to reduce the size of newspaper clippings and other printed matter. This practice saves lots of space and prevents the pages from looking overly cluttered. You could limit your scrapbook by representing a specific period of time, such as one year or one decade, depending on how avidly you go to the theater. Then try binders of a similar shape but in differing colors to create a theater or concert theme series.

As a cover or title page image, a photo or drawing of a proscenium arch can represent either theater or concerts. The traditional symbols of comedy and drama or musical notes are great representative cover images too.

For an interesting visual effect, try tracing the graphic symbols onto single-ply mat board, cutting them out, painting the shapes with acrylic paint, and gluing them to the surface. This raised imagery gives your cover or title page an unusual tactile quality.

TRAVEL SCRAPBOOK

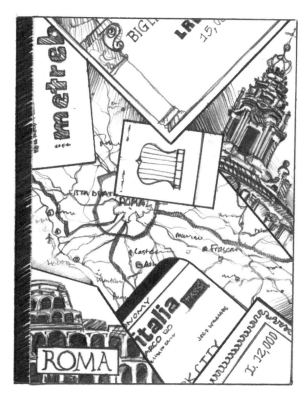

A travel scrapbook cover collage of ticket stubs, photos, and a map.

You might travel frequently for adventure or only occasionally for relaxation. But whatever your pleasure, a scrapbook preserving the trip will help you relive joyous moments and provide a good reference for future travel.

Your scrapbook can chronicle ten years of travel or a single destination. If you create your scrapbook during your trip, as a miniature diary, then the experiences can be captured with immediacy and vividness.

Travel journal ideas:

- *Pack a small, blank spiral-bound notebook (4" x 6", postcard size), a glue stick, tiny scissors, and a nice pen; each page of your scrapbook will contain a short record of the day's events during travel.*

- *Find an appropriate postcard and glue it on the front cover of the scrapbook to make it "official."*

- *Cut up an inexpensive map which indicates the locale of your hotel (or destination) and glue it to the back cover.*

- *Include travel confirmations and the unused portion of train or airline tickets.*

- *Buy postcards to document the places you visit (instantly you have photos).*

- *Stop at an automatic photo machine and mug it up.*

- *Save any printed matter from the day's activities: shopping bags, packaging, newspapers, concert programs, receipts, brochures, hotel stationery, maps, transportation schedules, business cards, restaurant cards, matchbooks,*

This travel journal scrapbook has a postcard glued on the cover of a spiral bound notebook. The scrapbooker also included a portion of ticket stub on her page of notes, handwritten during a vacation trip.

napkins, stamps, museum exhibit ticket stub.

Glue assorted paraphernalia like scraps of paper on which a native scribbled directions for you or the box of Chiclets with Arabic lettering; and write the relevant captions: "Ellen bought Chiclets to add a refreshing touch after our meal. To our surprise they were flavored with fennel! We visited the Villa Borghese on the Via Veneto today, and were lucky to get

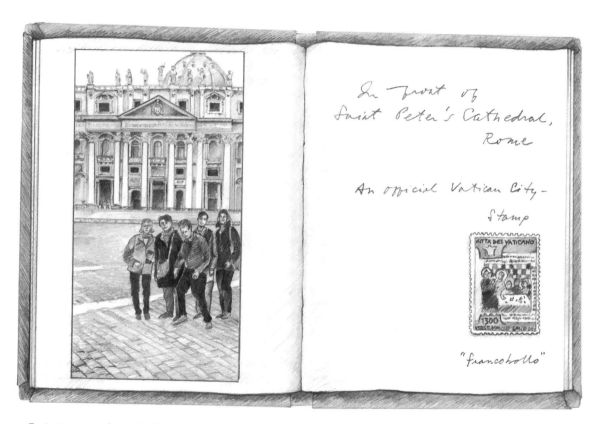

In front of
Saint Peter's Cathedral,
Rome

An official Vatican City-
Stamp

"francobollo"

An intimate travel scrapbook using a small cloth-bound book, cropped photograph, an actual stamp collected during the trip, and handwritten anecdotal information. An elegant little treasury.

tickets, it's the first season the museum has been open in 15 years!"

You can make another type of travel scrapbook after the trip. Gather materials suggested above and combine them with photos you have developed after you've arrived home.

For the cover and title of any travel scrapbook, use lettering found on postcards or hotel stationery. You can print your own lettering in a variety of typefaces on a computer. A photocopy enlargement of airline or train tickets lists time, dates, and destination and are enticing without giving away the visuals inside the book. Or consider a color copy enlargement of your passport.

A page from a travel journal describing a meal with drawings and notes.

A quintessential photograph or postcard of the trip makes an attractive visual title. Or try a photo montage that encourages picking up the scrapbook to see what all the photographs are about.

If you look for themes in your travel photographs, you will no doubt be inspired to create other scrapbooks.

- *Train rides scrapbook: photos of the trains, stations, and places. Add: ticket stubs, schedules.*

- *Great monuments scrapbook: Arc de Triomphe, Tomb of the Unknown Soldier, Mt. Rushmore, Taj Mahal.*

- *Renowned cathedrals, temples, synagogues.*

- *Natural wonders: Grand Canyon, Everglades, Rocky Mountains, Mississippi River.*

- *Skiing vacations scrapbook or beach vacations scrapbook.*

- *Favorite hotel scrapbook with brochures, cards, receipts, stationery, and photos of each establishment.*

WEDDING SCRAPBOOK

A satin ribbon-bound scrapbook with script lettering for romantic wedding memories.

A wedding is nearly equal to a birth as one of the most momentous and joyous milestones in a person's life. A scrapbook can preserve both the memory leading to the event and the utter delight of experiences on the special day. A wedding scrapbook does not compete with a formal photo album—instead the scrapbook can be a complement to the professional photos and include treasured items as well.

Professional photographers do a great job of getting just the right photos of the wedding event but often they are not around for the behind the scenes preparation. Here are some ideas for how to record the days leading up to your wedding:

- *Bring a camera along on the wedding gown search to photograph the dresses that were "maybes"—for surely, any bride is a bit wistful at turning away many worthy candidates in favor of the one absolutely perfect dress.*

- *Ask the florist to let you photograph the inside of the shop while the flowers are arranged.*

- *Photograph those small events that involve the wedding party and engagement period—don't forget to zoom-in for some close shots of surprised faces and teary-eyed parents and friends.*

- *Keep a small camera handy for pictures of the bride and groom shopping and planning for various aspects of the marriage: new furniture, invitations, picking out a ring.*

Mara Papa
and
Michael Gensinger
joyfully announce
their marriage
On Saturday, the 24 of November
Nineteen hundred and ninety four
at four-thirty in the afternoon.
La Jolla, California

Photos and other printed materials such as the wedding invitation can be reduced or enlarged photographically to create unique and interesting sizes for your scrapbook. A tiny scrapbook 4" x 5" is a private treasure, perhaps only for the eyes of the bride and groom.

Scrapbook pages might include:

- *The couple's courtship story: all the romantic details of where they met, where they went on dates, the proposal.*

- *Any pre-wedding or actual wedding day photographs.*

- *Photos cropped to fit the pages and to rid them of unwanted sections.*

- *A montage page with photos cut in interesting shapes: a photo of the wedding couple, for exam-*

Gifts

The Alomars	China settings
Betty Coleman	Antique serving dish
The Davis'	Ceramic bowl set
The Gibbs	Food processor
The Hargroves	Crystal glasses
The Rogers	Siverware
James Robinson	Crystal vase
The Smiths	China settings
The Williams	Sterling frame
Sue Workman	Monogram towels

Twenty years after your wedding, how do you remember what gifts you received or who sent a special card? A scrapbook is a good way to record details of your wedding that otherwise might be lost over time. At left, a collage of greeting cards and at right, a gift list.

ple, cut and fitted back together like two pieces of a puzzle, once separate but now complete.

- *The wedding invitation and several post-marked response cards with affirmative replies.*

- *Any printed materials such as the prayers, poems, or special words read at the ceremony. If there were extemporaneous remarks, you could print them yourself on a computer for the scrapbook—get that best man to write down his wedding toast.*

- *The dinner menu along with information about the chef or caterer and reception hall.*

- *A dinner napkin covered with signatures of the guests.*

- *A guest book page of salutations from all who participated. (Of course, a guest book can be a whole scrapbook in itself!)*

- *Telegrams sent as good wishes from those unable to attend.*

- *Wedding favors given to the guests. If they are too bulky, you can use a photograph of the favor.*

- *Pressed flowers made from the various arrangements.*

- *Sheet music of the songs played or performed.*

- *Receipts from all involved—your grandchildren will be amazed by the inexpensive costs of things in the "olden days!"*

- *A list of wedding presents with a collage of wrapping paper from the gifts.*

- *Whole wedding cards or cards cut up and arranged into a collage.*

- *A photocopy of the marriage license.*

- *The masthead from the local newspaper with the wedding date.*

The wedding scrapbook itself might echo the colors, textures, and style of the wedding. Did you have a formal affair? Your scrapbook could reflect the classic style of your wedding by using an elegant covering and beautiful 100 percent cotton paper interior and hand-marbleized end papers.

Was your wedding a casual event on the beach or backyard? Your scrapbook could have a free flowing arrangement. Did you wear antique clothing at your wedding? Use a tapestry or leather cover with calligraphy for your scrapbook to look like antique binding and lettering.

If you'd like to recall the elegance of the wedding gown after it has been carefully tucked away, consider this tip: contact the manufacturer of your wedding dress and ask for a yard of the fabric. Cover your scrapbook with the fabric or simply put a piece on a scrapbook page next to a photo of the bride.

Other wedding scrapbook ideas:

- *Wedding guest scrapbook, which includes guest signatures, good wishes, cards, and photos.*

- *A scrapbook of the bride's and groom's childhood, including baby photos and other memorabilia. This makes a great engagement gift for the couple.*

- *A virtual wedding scrapbook. In this digital age, you can preserve memories and share them with everyone you know who has a computer. How? By creating a virtual scrapbook on the World Wide Web and later transferring it to a CD-ROM. You can have an interactive web site before the wedding and add to it after the event.*

Web pages might include:

- *A photograph of the wedding couple and the wedding announcement.*

- *Baby pictures of the couple.*

- *A guest book.*

- *Travel information for guests.*

- *A brief history of the couple.*

- *A gift registry.*

- *Photographs of all sorts.*

- *A video clip.*

- *Audio clips.*

*A*cross the years: *an eleven-year-old's scrapbook made from construction paper tied with ribbon juxtaposed against her mother's junior high scrapbook from the 1960s. Once the daughter discovered it, she tore off a corner of a blank page and pasted it in her own scrapbook with the caption, "This is from a scrapbook Mom kept in middle school. Two generations!"*

PARTFIVE: SCRAPBOOK
SOCIALS

The best advice I can give to readers is that a finished book is great, but the process is the purer joy.

— Rose Gonnella,
Scrapbook Guild

The New Quilting Bees

In many ways, scrapbooking seems a solitary art. Mostly on your own, you search through closets, sort through photos, and scribble down memories. Soon you realize, however, that very little about scrapbooking involves only one person.

In scrapbooking, we locate pictures of our loved ones, ask questions of our relatives, even get our friends or children to help us shop for supplies. Physically putting a scrapbook together may be a one-person event, but the entire process can be a collective effort. Not surprisingly, then, as scrapbooks become important to more and more lives, enthusiasm for this cherished craft has created a phenomenon comparable to the quilting bees of the 19th century.

Victorian women often gathered for quilting parties, known as "quiltings" or "quilting bees" to pursue their creative arts and catch up on the local goings on. Today, women facing the challenges of the 21st century turn to scrapbooking "crops" and clubs for the same reasons. Across the country, women and occasionally men gather to work on their current scrapbooks, glean ideas from others, share supplies, or just catch up on the interesting lives in their communities.

The Four Cs of Scrapbooking

Scrapbooking is contagious fun and spreads quickly and joyfully to others. If you remember the Four Cs of "social" scrapbooking—Clubs, Crops, Classes, and Cruises—you'll find valuable resources for meeting others in the field. Inspiration and community-building aside, the Four Cs can help you in many practical ways—sharing or buying supplies, learning new techniques, moving creativity to the next level.

First, consider a club. It's an informal, relaxed way to get together with friends and enjoy the craft. The main advantage? It's free. You'll find companions who can inspire you with their work or nurse you through the more tedious tasks. Stuck on a page? Use layouts and designs your friends have created as a springboard to set you soaring again. If someone else has a paper punch you've been meaning to try, just borrow it. You'll save money and come out ahead creatively.

If you don't know of a club in your area, consider starting one. Or check out the local scrapbookers' area of your favorite on-line scrapbook site. (See *Resource Section* on page 242 for suggested sites.) You might also call local craft or scrapbooking stores—they may leap at the chance to sponsor your club . . . and to cultivate a few steady customers. Remember that clubs rarely offer specific presentations of ideas and information, as do crops and classes. Also, if you run out of supplies, you can't buy more, like you can at a crop where a scrapbook company or store may sponsor the event. Crops offer access to new products and a chance to learn about them before buying. Should you decide to buy, products are often discounted. Classes and workshops will help you with a specific topic, such as layout or journal writing. Professional crops, classes, and workshops usually require a fee for demonstrations on a particular aspect of scrapbooking.

If you really want to go "overboard" with scrapbooking, you can even sign up for a scrapbooking convention at sea. Scrapbook Guild member Jennia Hart hosts an annual cruise, transforming an entire ship into a scrapbooker's version of heaven—with classes, workshops, seminars, tools, and supplies. One year they set their sights on Mexico, another year Puerto Rico and St. Thomas. For more information about this true specialty vacation, contact Jennia on her Internet site, The Scrapbooking Idea Network, www.scrapbooking.com.

How to Hold a Scrapbooking Bee

If the social aspect of scrapbooking seems sweet as honey to you, host a bee of your own. Just like putting on any party, you'll need to do a bit of planning first. Ask yourself: Do I want to have just a few friends over to crop and paste? Or do I want to get to know lots of new people?

If you're leaning toward casually inviting a few friends, then plan as you would any party. Send invitations, buy refreshments, etc. Just make sure you have one big or several small tables that friends can use to spread out scrapbook materials. Keep refreshments simple. In fact, a separate room entirely makes sense, since food and scrapbooks don't mix well on the same table. Call it the risk of ruin.

If you prefer a full-scale gathering, consider using a church or community center for the event. In either case, remind guests in your invitations to bring their own supplies and materials. (See *Tips for Scrapbooking Away from Home* on page 235 for supplies to suggest.)

More on Clubs

Here are some great pointers on clubs from Scrapbook Guild member Jennia Hart:

Money. The number one reason that scrapbookers want to form a scrapbooking club is to save money. Tired of paying for table space to work on their scrapbook, scrapbookers all over the country are forming scrapbooking clubs to enable them to get together for free and scrapbook with others. Scrapbooking clubs can share resources and even babysitters.

Friendship. High on the list of reasons to start a club is friendship. Getting together with others to scrapbook is a good way to make new friends in your area. Most scrapbookers share many common traits including creativity, love of their family, and the desire to preserve their family history. Quilting bees were not events that one paid for and scrapbooking shouldn't have to be either.

Learning new techniques. Many groups hire a guest speaker to provide instruction. One local group has the same company representative come monthly to provide instruction and materials for a two-page seasonal layout. The scrapbookers, who pay a $5 fee, feel that it is well worth it to learn a new stamping technique and use the materials provided by the instructor. Some clubs distribute handouts or have a member of the group speak on a new technique.

Announce your club online. The local scrapbookers area of The Scrapbooking Idea Network is an excellent place to start. Your free listing can tell potential members where you meet, who to contact, and how much, if any, fee there is to join. Bulletin boards and listservers can also serve as a way to get the word out.

Friends. Invite your scrapbooking friends to join you to scrapbook. This is how most existing clubs got started.

Mother's groups. Be sure to let your children's playmates' parents know that you are forming a scrapbooking club. Everyone has photos and joining a scrapbooking club may be just what they need to get started on that backlog of family photos.

Local scrapbooking stores. They may be willing to let you leave flyers at the store and they may even be willing to host the club meetings.

Organizing Your Club

How many members do you want in your club? When you are starting the club you may want to think about your goals for the club. Do you want to invest a minimum of

Jody Williams (Scrapbook Guild) takes a travel vacation every year with her best friend. One year, when her friend couldn't make it, Jody went to Italy on her own. She created this scrapbook, including the handmade book itself, as a gift for the friend she left behind. A charming little narrative story accompanies the simple snapshots, mounted one to a page for maximum impact.

By chance, I ended up on
castel strada.

This one: chiuso,

time in the club? Then maybe keeping the number of members to a minimum and meeting in members' houses is the best plan for you. Are you willing to invest some time and effort into organizing the club, meeting places, speakers, etc.? Then maybe a large group that can pay for a meeting place and speakers should be your goal. Each group will have different dynamics depending on its member base. You will need to determine what goals your group has and make your decisions based on your group's preferences. Larger clubs may need to have a formal structure and even elected officers in place to function well.

No matter how small your club is, be sure to delegate to the members equally. Tasks can be assigned on a volunteer basis, by drawing names or simply by drawing on the members' strengths. Delegating the tasks helps keep the club a pleasure for all involved.

Where to meet? Homes, scrapbooking/craft stores, churches, community centers, and even the workplace are all popular locations. Every meeting location choice has pro and cons to be considered. When choosing a location think about lighting, room and table space, safety at night after the meeting, availability of a kitchen, parking, distance for the members to drive, availability of a child care area (if needed), and cost. Another consideration is mixing business with pleasure. While it is convenient for members to be able to purchase items during the meeting, if there are several consultants or retailers in the club it may not work out well. Think through the commercial aspects carefully before committing to meet at a scrapbooking or crafts store.

How to schedule or announce meetings? Will your club meet regularly? One club meets every other Friday in the same member's home. This makes it easy for everyone to remember what night it is and eliminates the need for any formal newsletter or notification system. An e-mail reminder is sent the week of the meeting with pertinent information. Many rubber stamping clubs have newsletters or send postcards to announce meetings.

How much should the dues be? This will depend greatly on the group dynamics mentioned above. If your group wants to have guest speakers, rent a room to meet, send newsletters, etc., then dues will be necessary in order to fund these things. Many scrapbooking groups have decided to be "fee free" as getting away from fees was the primary motivation for starting the scrapbooking club.

Different scrapbooking clubs provide amazingly diverse activities for members. Demonstrations, classes, sharing, working on scrapbooks, and eating and/or drinking (away from the albums, of course) are all popular. Some clubs provide handouts or do swaps in addition to their other activities. What your club wants and needs will depend on how your club operates. Small clubs that simply want to work on albums will not need much of an agenda. Larger clubs and clubs that provide speakers will want to have an agenda so that the speaker will have enough time to convey her information to the group. Many rubber stamping clubs are quite formal and even participate in community projects and fundraisers. If your club decides to go this route, a formal structure will be necessary to keep the members up-to-date on the club's progress.

A Family and Friends Activity

Scrapbooking can be a form of communication. Family members who scrapbook together are keeping up the ties that bind. Friends far away can pass scrapbooks back and forth, each adding their own personalities to the book. They compile an ever-changing record of friendship, a living history of shared lives.

You gather around the kitchen table with your family to put together the ultimate Grand Canyon vacation scrapbook. Or you spend a weekend away with your sisters sorting through decades of ancestors' photos. Wherever, however it's done, scrapbooking adds up in the end to more than the sum of its pages.

Scrapbook Guild member Rose Gonnella exchanges scrapbooks with fellow Guild member and friend Jody Williams. Sometimes they exchange a photocopy, but they also give each other original books and collaborate on some projects.

"While I was visiting Jody at her home in Minnesota," Rose recalls, "we had the idea to make a little book commemorating all the travel we had done together. It became our 'Trips So Far' scrapbook. Jody made the paper for the inside. We bought the paper for the cover on a trip to Florence, Italy. We made tiny symbolic drawings, then Jody turned them into etchings. The binding is an accordion fold, so it opens up completely and gives the whole view at once or page by page. It is so cute . . . everyone wants one. But only a handful were made, and we save them for special gifts."

"Trips So Far" can be admired on page 229.

On-line Allies

The only scrapbooker with a reason to be solitary is the one who wants it that way. In fact, an enthusiastic scrapbook community is as close as your computer. The Internet has emerged as a great resource for information about classes, workshops, and conventions in your area. It can link you to other scrapbookers, invariably eager to communicate all they know about this exciting craft. You even view an almost infinite number of real layout ideas.

On several Internet sites, you can participate in "live chats" or conversations with other scrapbook artisans. If you've never tried it, don't worry. It's really pretty simple. You enter a chat area for a certain site, type in a nickname, then write your message. Other people in the chat room at the time see your message, and they can respond immediately. It's a great way to get answers to questions and find new ideas.

Some Internet sites have regularly scheduled monthly chats as well as round-the-clock chat rooms. All the fascinating possibilities of the Internet can be applied to your craft—electronically, you'll meet friends from around the world who share your interests and aims.

Scrapbook Party

Scrapbooks make a fine excuse for all kinds of parties. They also make a wonderful theme.

Plan just about any holiday party with scrapbooking in mind. Why not a Fourth of July reunion, complete with albums, paper, scissors, and photos and bunting, of course? How about a pre-Christmas or Hanukkah party, as a way to finish up those scrapbooks you'd like to give as gifts? A Scrapbook Makeover party could bring lots of friends together to update, overhaul, and spruce up those old crumbling or "magnetic" albums—the super 8mm. home movies of the scrapbooking world.

Guild member Jody Williams helped turn an ordinary wedding shower into a marvelous memory by compiling a scrapbook during the party. She created a handmade, paper-covered book designed to match the wedding invitations. She brought the book to the shower, along with an instant camera, scissors, and a glue stick. She recorded each gift in the book, added bits of ribbon and wrapping paper, and slipped in the cards that accompanied the gifts. She included a business card from the restaurant, one of the centerpiece flowers, quickly pressed, and wishes and predictions for the bride and groom.

The instant camera proved an inspiration. Guests took pictures of each other, the food, the flower arrangement . . . and even the waiter, who signed an inscription for the bride in the book next to his photo.

"Everyone enjoyed participating," Jody recalls, "the book was passed from person to person, and was quite in demand. The group activity turned an ordinary shower into a very lively party."

Love and Charity

We cannot do great things in life; we can only do small things with great love.

— Mother Teresa

The quilting bees of the 19th century evolved into sewing circles in local churches, then into larger social groups. Many nights after a quilting, the husbands and other family members would arrive for a potluck dinner and dance. Charity also thrived through the craft of quilting. Colorful quilts would be lovingly stitched at group gatherings, then raffled off to raise money for the needy. Such activities lie at the heart of nostalgia, the very essence of "the good old days" in our country.

Such communal traditions could easily be translated into scrapbook traditions for our own times. After a Saturday morning crop, families could gather for a summer picnic or a softball game. Group scrapbooks could be auctioned to raise money for school equipment, a homeless shelter, or an environmental project. And after you're caught up on your own scrapbooks, why not volunteer your time and extra supplies to youth groups? They could learn to appreciate the value of tradition and creativity through scrapbooking projects. Some day, with luck, the times we live in could be their "good old days."

Tips for Scrapbooking Away from Home

Scrapbooker Maureen Guretzski came away a bit disappointed from her first scrapbooking group. She expected it to be a sort of class, a place where she would learn more about scrapbooking, not simply put pages together. Still, eager to try it again, she got into the swing of things and the second time "whipped out pages." She says planning made the difference from one session to the next. Her suggestion: line up what you want to work on during the week before. Then you can "really motor" when you get there.

Whether you are attending a workshop, a crop, a cruise, or just spending a few days at your parents' house to catch up on some journal writing, Maureen's suggestion is useful: plan ahead.

Presort the photos you will use. Label them in envelopes. Think about the layouts you wish to complete. Decide what colors or types of paper you may need. Pack a few necessary tools—sharp scissors, your choice of adhesive, a good supply of paper. Include one or two extras—decorative scissors, rubber stamps, stickers—if you think they might inspire you. A file box with a handle is a convenient carrying case. Planning will definitely make your work away from home more productive and pleasurable.

Meanwhile, whether you're home or away, we in the Scrapbook Guild wish you luck and wish you well. Happy Scrapbooking!

The bride gave this elegant scrapbook to her bridesmaid after the wedding photographs were developed. The use of black and white photographs cropped in a square to echo the square-shaped, handmade album adds to its simple beauty.

PART SIX: # RESOURCE SECTION

Being informed is your best assurance of getting the products that you want for your scrapbook.

— Marie Nuccitelli,
Scrapbook Guild

General

Creative Memories
P.O. Box 1839
St. Cloud, MN 56301
800-468-9335

Creating Keepsakes
P.O. Box 1106
Orem, UT 84059
801-224-8235

Lark Books Catalog
67 Broadway
Asheville, NC 28801
800-284-3388

Books

Affirmations for Artists
by Eric Maisel, PhD.
Putnam Publishing Group, 1996

Collage from Seeds, Leaves, and Flowers
by Joan Carver
Guild of Mastercraftsmen, 1997

Cover to Cover
by Shereen LaPlantz
Sterling Publishers, 1998

Creative Bookbinding
by Pauline Johnson
Dover Publications, 1990

Familiar Quotations
by John Bartlett
Little, Brown and Company, 1968

The History of Printed Scraps
    by Alistair Allen and Joan Hoverstadt
    New Cavendish Books, 1983

Japanese Bookbinding
    by Kojiro Ikegami
    Weatherhill, 1986

Nature Printing With Herbs, Fruits, and Flowers
    by Laura Donnelly Bethmann
    Storey Books, 1996

Non-Adhesive Binding
    by Keith A. Smith
    Visual Studies Workshop Press, 1995

The Oxford Dictionary of Quotations
    Angela Partington, Ed.
    Oxford University Press, 1996

Photomontage
    by Stephen Golding
    Rockport Publishers, 1997

Scrap-Books and How To Make Them
    by E.W. Gurley
    The Author's Publishing Company, 1880

The Wordsworth Dictionary of Proverbs
    by G.L. Apperson
    Wordsworth Editions Ltd, 1997

Web Sites

Ask an Expert
http://www.mnhs.org/prepast/
conserve/photopres.html

Common Threads
http://www.gensource.com/
common/index.htm

Crypted and Sunni
http://www.customeffects.com

DMarie
http://dmarie.com

E-Signature
http://www.e-signature.com/
english/english.htm

Fontastic
http://rover.wiesbaden.netsurf.de/kikita

Font Empire
http://fontempire.host4u.com

4 Research Help
http://www.4researchhelp.com/help

Free Font Fiesta
http://members.aol.com/mmqchome/
fonts/fonts.htm

Graceful Bee
http://www.gracefulbee.com/index.html

I Found It!
Genealogy Search Engine
http://www.gensource.com/ifoundit/
index.htm

Memories Expo
http://www.creative-industries.com/
memories

Preserving Memories
http://www.lib.cmich.edu/clarke/
pres.htm

Scrapbooking Obsession
http://www.geocities.com/Heartland/
Ranch/2637/#Chats

Scrap Happy
http://www/telepath.com/bcarson/
scrap_happy

Scrap Net
http://www.netprojections.com/
scrapnet/scrapnet.htm

Sing a Song
http://mypage.direct.ca/f/fstringe/
sing1.html#B128

The International Lyrics Server
http://www/lyrics.ch

Top 40 Lyrics
http://www.summer.com.br/pfilho/
html/top40/index.html

Scrapbook Supplies

3M-Scotch
3M Bldg. 221-5N-38
De Paul, MN 55144

All My Memories
Mission Trace Center
3355 S. Yarrow, Suite E-127
Lakewood, CO 80227
303-986-2200
and
7721 Wadsworth Blvd.
Arvada, CO 80003
303-456-7616

Artistic Albums & More
P.O. Box 5123-416
El Toro, CA 92630
714-888-7038

Crafter's Toy Box
P.O. Box 282
Larkspur, CO 80118
800-797-2197

Crafty Cutter
179 Niblick Road Suite #344
Paso Robles, CA 93446
805-237-7833

Forever Memories
2024 Nut Tree Road
Vacaville, CA 95687
707-455-7760

Gick
9 Studebaker Drive
Irvine, CA 92718

Kozy Memories
6006 Marsh Hawk Ct.
Elk Grove, CA 95758
916-683-5090

Liquid Paper
Box 621 Gillette
Boston, MA 02199

Memories Direct
P.O. Box 1053
Fremont, NE 86026
402-721-5800

Memory By Design
1771 N. Main Street #4
Layton, UT 84041
801-775-9380

Moore Creations
P.O. Box 4156
Mission Viejo, CA 92690
714-249-5397

Pebbles in My Pocket
P.O. Box 1506
Orem, UT 84059-1506
800-438-8153

Plaid
1649 International Court
Norcross, GA 30091
770-923-8200

Remember When…
607 Gregory Lane #150
Pleasant Hill, CA 94523
925-938-1700

Scrapbook Company Catalog
1115 North 200 East, Suite 140
Logan, UT 84341
888-750-6844

Scrappers Unlimited Catalog
P.O. Box 337
Eureka, MO 63025

Scrappin' & Stampin'
33221 Plymouth
Livonia, MI 48150
313-266-3014

Stamp DeVille
1014 S. Broadway Suite 100
Carrollton, TX 75006
972-245-5755

Timeless Treasures
22411 Antonio Parkway C-160
Rancho Santa Margarita, CA 92688
714-888-7151

Albums

Bombay Company
P.O. Box 161009
Fort Worth, TX 76161
800-829-7789

BookMakers
6001 66th Ave. #101
Riverdale, MD 20737
301-459-3384

Cachet
300 Fairfield Rd.
Fairfield, NJ 07004
973-882-8400

C.R. Gibson
32 Knight St.
Norwalk, CT 06856
203-847-4543

Exposures
P.O. Box 3615
Oshkosh, WI 54903
800-572-5750

Flax
240 Valley Drive
Brisbane, CA 94005
800-547-7778

Hiller
631 North 400 West
Salt Lake City, UT 84103
801-521-2411

Kate's Paperie
561 Broadway
New York, NY 10012
800-809-9880

Kodak
343 State Street
Rochester, NY 14650
315-253-1486

Light Impressions
P.O. Box 940
Rochester, NY 14603
800-828-6216

Pioneer Photo Albums
9801 Deering Avenue
Chatsworth, CA 91311
818-873-1573

Restoration Source
P.O. Box 9384
Salt Lake City, UT 84109-0384
801-278-7880

905 Studio
90 Rock Ridge Road
Upper Black Eddy, PA 18972
800-905-6556

Paper

Aiko's Art Materials
3347 North Clark St.
Chicago, IL 60657
773-404-5600

Canson Acid-Free Papers
21 Industrial Dr.
South Hadley, MA 01085
413-538-9250

Flax
(see Albums for address)

Hot Off the Press
1250 NW Third, Dept. CK4
Canby, OR 97013
503-266-9102

Kate's Paperie
(see Albums for address)

Paper Access
23 West 18th Street
New York, NY 10011
212-463-7035

Paper Direct
100 Plaza Drive
Secaucus, NJ 07094
800-272-7377

Photographic Restoration

American Institute for
Conservation of Historic
and Artistic Works
1717 K Street, NW Suite 301
Washington, D.C. 20006
202-452-9545

Archival Company
P.O. Box 1239
Northampton, MA 01061-1239
800-442-7576

The Iowa Conservation and
Preservation Consortium
c/o State Historical Society of Iowa
402 Iowa Avenue
Iowa City, IA 52240
FAX 319-335-3935

Kate's Paperie
(see Albums for address)

The South Carolina Department
of Archives and History
8361 Parkland Rd.
Columbia, SC 29223
803-896-6211

State Historical Society
of North Dakota
612 East Blvd.
Bismarck, ND 58505
701-328-2668

Rubber Stamps

Flax
(see Albums for address)

Graphic Rubber Stamp
818-762-9443

Hampton Art Stamps
19 Industrial Blvd.
Medford, NY 11763
516-924-1335

Hero Arts
1343 Powell St,
Emeryville, CA 94608
510-652-6055

Inkadinkado
60 Cummings Park
Woburn, MA 01801
781-938-6100

Mostly Animals
  P.O. Box 2355
  Oakdale, CA 95361
  209-848-2542

Posh Impressions
  4708 Barranca Parkway
  Irvine, CA 92604
  714-651-1145

Stamp Cabana
  352 Park Avenue South
  Winter Park, FL 32789
  407-628-8863

Stampendous Inc.
  1357 South Lewis Street
  Anaheim, CA 92805
  714-563-9501

Scissors & Other Cutting Equipment

Accu-Cut Shape and Letter
Cutting Systems
  P.O. Box 1053
  Fremont, NE 68025
  800-288-1670

Fiskars
  7811 West Stewart Ave.
  Wausau, WI 54401
  715-842-2091

Flax
  (see Albums for address)

Uchida of America
  3535 Del Amo Blvd.
  Torrance, CA 90503
  310-793-2200

INDEX